# It Hasteth Away

An Island Wife and Her Soldier Husband
A Civil War Story

By
Randy Purinton

Copyright © 2010  Randy Purinton
All rights reserved.

ISBN: 1452893810
ISBN-13: 9781452893815
Library of Congress Control Number: 2010907813

*"Be ye also ready."*

—Sabrina Brown to Lucinda Seeley, 1862, from the Gospel of Matthew, chapter 24, verse 44

# ACKNOWLEDGMENTS

Islesboro Historical Society volunteer archivists Bunny Logan and Marcie Congdon were very helpful in providing me with access to the correspondence researched for this book.

I thank Charlie Pendleton and Pendleton Stevens – great-grandsons of Sabrina Seeley Brown Pendleton – for sharing their family's history. I also thank my former college English teacher, Richard D'Abate, Executive Director of the Maine Historical Society, for his advice. My wife, Anita, was a source of unrelenting encouragement and support.

The book SECOND TO NONE by James H. Mundy provided a useful, fascinating and detailed history of the Second Maine Volunteer Infantry.

# CONTENTS

Preface ................................................................... 1
Letters .................................................................... 5
Islesboro ............................................................... 13
Sabrina Seeley ..................................................... 17
Courtship............................................................. 25
Mother ................................................................. 45
Sabrina Seeley Brown ........................................ 51
Enlistment And Departure.................................53
First Manassas .................................................... 61
Gossip .................................................................. 71
The Court Of Death............................................ 81
Something Like Sex ............................................83
"... the vicissitudes of a soldier's life..." ........... 87
Second Manassas: The Court Of Death......... 115
Timetable To Hell ............................................. 117
Widowhood........................................................137
Sabrina Seeley Brown Pendleton ................... 147
Epilogue..............................................................151

# PREFACE

This is the story behind the letters between Sabrina and Wesley Brown of Islesboro, Maine, married for one month before Wesley enlisted in the Union Army and never returned. This is also a love story that is preserved in the correspondence between husband and wife. Sabrina stored the letters in her house, Gablewood on Islesboro, in which she lived for many years with her second husband, Fields Coombs Pendleton. Sabrina's second daughter, Alice Lavinia Pendleton, assumed possession of her mother's letters and papers because, of Sabrina's seven children, Alice seemed to be the most interested in her family's history.

For many years, Alice's papers and the letters were among her personal belongings in the family's house at 250 83$^{rd}$ Street in the Bay Ridge section of Brooklyn, where Alice's brother, Fields Seeley Pendleton, Sr. (son of Sabrina and Fields Coombs Pendleton), moved the family.

Alice Pendleton, her sisters, and family summered at Gablewood on Islesboro. It may be that Alice herself brought the correspondence back to the island with her and kept it there. As Alice and her sisters passed on, it seems likely that Alice's niece—also named Alice—became the owner of her aunt's papers. When she married Clifford Purse, she became Alice Purse, and when Gablewood was sold out of the Pendleton family, Alice Purse became the custodian of Alice Pendleton's papers. She and her husband owned an estate on what is known as Northeast Point, which faces East Penobscot Bay and looks across Broad Cove to Hewes Point. That's

*Gablewood before the existing, wrap-around porch was installed. Islesboro Historical Society.*

where the letters were stored for many years. Pendleton Stevens—Alice Purse's nephew and also Sabrina Seeley Brown Pendleton's great-grandson—inherited that estate and the papers in it. He donated papers of Alice L. Pendleton that are archived in the Islesboro Historical Society, including the correspondence between Sabrina and Wesley Brown.

The reason this book contains segments of those letters is because Sabrina's great-grandson Pendleton Stevens donated his aunt Alice L. Pendleton's papers and the letters to the Islesboro Historical Society, material that Alice Purse—Alice L. Pendleton's niece—once had in her possession and stored in her house on Northeast

Point. The letters were stored in a box in that house and were donated along with the bulk of Alice's papers—including notes related to an island history she once wanted to write—and were then sorted and archived.

I became familiar with the letters because I wanted to write an article about a Civil War correspondence but I don't remember why except that I knew that books about the topic interested people who loved Maine history and who admired Colonel Joshua Chamberlain, a Maine native and hero at the battle of Gettysburg. So I marched up the stairs of the Islesboro Historical Society and asked the first staffer I met—Bunny Logan, archivist—if there was a Civil War correspondence in the Society's archives. She responded, "Why, yes. We have the correspondence between Sabrina Seeley and Wesley Brown!" That was the beginning of my research. The story behind the people in those letters is the subject of this book.

# LETTERS

If the greatest literature is praiseworthy because critics say that it expresses the truth of human experience then war correspondence deserves the same consideration. Letters written between soldiers and their loved ones often reveal poignant and powerful expressions of drama and passion. Reading this correspondence can move us to consider whether or not we would feel and think in the same ways as someone who lived long ago. Reflecting on the motives of our ancestors' behaviors is not just a process that offers interest and amusement; it teaches us what feelings and thoughts are important to all people throughout history. We can critique the content of our own lives against the lives of those who are long gone and decide for ourselves whether or not the past is so much different than the present. We might learn lessons about ourselves. Letters are powerful literature not because the correspondents are trying to create the experience of love, absence, and loss for a novel or script; they *are* the experience.

Often an exchange of letters concludes when a soldier returns home, but there's no guarantee a soldier will return and sometimes the exchange simply ends. Then we know that behind the correspondence there was great conflict and suffering. It may be the survivor who suffers the most because she retains the memory of departure, absence, death, and loss.

Ernest Hemingway was an ambulance driver for Allied forces during World War I. He would be among the first civilians to enter an area that was the site of a recent battle. Always upon entering the battlefield, Hemingway was struck by the abundance of paper that surrounded the corpses and blew across the wasted and battered landscape. He wrote, "These were the new dead and no one had bothered with anything but their pockets. Their coats had been opened and their pockets were out. There was always much paper about the dead, the letters, letters, letters."

It was the same during the American Civil War. Both corpses and paper littered the field in the aftermath of battle. It is likely that the papers escaped their owners' pockets and backpacks during the looting of bodies that occurred as the victors rifled through the clothing of the vanquished, searching for anything of value, whether it was ammunition, money, boots, or simply a souvenir. Paper had the least value so it was ignored and discarded. Left to drift and tumble across the blasted landscape, thousands of letters lodged against broken fence posts and carriage wheels, shattered trees and mangled hedges until the rains came, washed the ink into the soil, and soaked the paper so that it dissolved and became one with the earth.

When a soldier dies, a correspondence ends and the person at the other end of that correspondence will mourn not only the loss of her soldier but also the loss of an activity that was her sole—or soul—link to her absent love.

Wesley Brown, twenty-two, had an active correspondence with his wife, Sabrina Brown, twenty, nicknamed Brina, who was formerly Sabrina Seeley, of Islesboro, Maine. Both wrote dozens of letters to each other during the sixteen months that Wesley was in the Union Army. Sometimes it took a week for a letter to travel between mid-coast Maine and Washington, D.C. Sometimes

*Sabrina, probably in her early twenties. Islesboro Historical Society.*

the letters never reached their destination. Mail was tampered with, too. Soldiers would send home portions of their meager salaries, providing dishonest mail personnel opportunities to open envelopes and pocket the contents. In January 1862, Wesley wrote Sabrina a letter explaining how a portion of his monthly salary would, in the future, be wired by the government to a local Maine bank for her to withdraw at her convenience:

*Camp Jameson Halls Hill Va.*
   *January 13th 1862*
   *...I have signed an allotment roll, whereby eight dollars per month of my wages is secured to you commencing Jan 1st 1862. It will be sent to you at the end of every two months (i.e.) when we are paid off. The reason of my doing so was that it was safer than to trust it to letters and sometimes we may be where I could not send it...I should have signed more but I wish to keep some by me so in case I am taken prisoner to have something to buy a dinner with...*

In a letter dated November 30, 1861, Wesley responds in anger to Sabrina's concern that he might be low on envelopes because on arrival his last letter looked like it had been mangled:

*You say that my letter of the 17th looked as if I was short of envelopes. Well, I was not and that one left me in as good shape as any of them does, and I think that it must have been broken open and I want you to send that letter [back to me], won' t you. Do not fail as I want to know just what was in it, every word. I would like to know if Capt. Sprague breaks open every letter that comes into his hands. If I knew of his opening one of my letters that was directed to you he might receive a hint to attend to his own business and pay a few of his debts and so forth ere he tries to find out what I choose to write to my Brina wife. Any person who would do that is not fit to live among civilized beings. But perhaps Capt. Sprague, Capt. Redman and a few others I might name cannot find any other employment than in prying into other people's affairs. I believe it is congenial to their nature, and they had better enlist in the army for that purpose, as the government pays a very good price to all who are deft in that art. But enough of such stuff. How do you do and what are you doing? What do you find to employ yourself about all the time. You need not knit me any more socks as I now have four pair and they are good ones and will last me a long time.*

Captain Sprague was probably William P. Sprague, who was born on Islesboro in 1835. Nineteenth-century Islesboro island historian Joseph Pendleton Farrow described him as a merchant and postmaster of North Islesboro, the area where Sabrina Brown lived. William P. Sprague was twenty-six years old and eligible for the draft when Wesley wrote the above letter. Captain Sprague paid a commutation fee and avoided the war altogether. Captain Benjamin Redman also paid the commutation fee after being drafted. The Union draft began in July 1863, the same month that the Battle of Gettysburg was fought. Wesley died months before Sprague and Redman were drafted and were privileged not to serve the Union, as Wesley chose, so he wasn't disgusted at the two men for their lack of patriotism. Evidently, Wesley had other reasons not to like them.

If the suspicion that his mail was being tampered with by men he disliked wasn't enough to poison Wesley's mood, he discovered soon after enlisting that he wouldn't have enough room in his backpack to save all of the correspondence that he was receiving from relatives and especially Sabrina. His letter dated October 19, 1861, a little more than five months after he enlisted, explains why so few of Sabrina's letters survive in the collection, compared to the number of Wesley's letters that Sabrina saved:

*It gives me much pain to destroy my letters, especially those from you, but I am obliged to do so about once a month as I have no place to keep them. So darling you must write me real heart letters, and let me know all your joys and sorrows, won't you dearest wife. Write a dozen sheets a week, but as I cannot I'll close hoping to hear from you often and that you will write real long letters. Your devoted husband as ever, Wesley Brown.*

In her last letter to Wesley, Sabrina wrote that she sent half a dozen letters to her husband after he was freed from incarceration in Richmond but Wesley complained that she hadn't written any to him. Sabrina was sending letters but her letters just weren't getting to Wesley. And the sad truth is that fewer of her letters survived because Wesley burned them. In his letter describing his role in the battle of First Manassas, Wesley wrote, "*Before the battle I would have wagered my life that we should conquer but it was not to be. For fear of your letters being seen by someone else in case I was shot I burnt every one of them and since that time have felt lonesome on that account, so darling you must write a lot to make up for those won't you."*

Sabrina suggested that Wesley send the letters back to her.

Wesley never thought of doing that: "*It was painful for me to burn your loved letters but the idea of sending them home never entered my thick skull. So darling, you see, that was the reason why I burned them.*" Because the correspondence contains letters from both husband and wife, we know that Wesley took Sabrina' advice to heart and conscientiously returned her letters in the same envelopes that he used to send his own letters to her.

Even before Wesley left Maine with the Second Maine Volunteer Infantry, he knew that his marriage was going to be defined by the frequency and quality of the correspondence between himself and Sabrina. Still in Bangor and on the eve of departure, Wesley wrote, "*...darling if I could see you I would cheerfully give all the pay that I shall make while I am gone but as that is impossible we must do the next best thing (i.e.) write as often as we can.*" Wesley cherished his marriage and his correspondence with his wife. He would not allow the integrity of Sabrina's letters to be put at risk of being compromised by the uncaring eyes of dishonest handlers, strangers, and enemies. Sabrina felt the same way about the letters from Wesley that she saved in a trunk. Several months after Wesley's death, Sabrina tells Luky, her sister, that she can go through the trunk to check if there was anything that suited her needs but that she was not to breach her privacy by inspecting the contents of the envelopes that contained her correspondence: *"Don't take them out of the chest, will you, Luky. They are letters from Wesley and as such are sacred to me."*

The correspondence, then, is not complete, but not because Sabrina's descendants were careless or lost any of it. We are privileged to have about half of its original content and that includes letters from both husband and wife over a period of about two and a half years.

# ISLESBORO

It was from the third generation of islanders that Islesboro filled its quota of recruits for the Union Army. The old settlers, those who first settled the island in the 1770s and '80s, died off early in the nineteenth century. The second generation built sloops and schooners for Islesboro mariners, many of whom fished and freighted lumber and coal. The last schooner built on the island was the *Mary Jane*, in 1830.

Early in the years of settlement, Islesboro, in the middle of Penobscot Bay, was called Long Island because it is much longer than it is wider. There was a time when Islesboro might have been two islands instead of one but now the island looks pinched in the middle like an hourglass. So there's the northern part of the island, which is across the water from Castine in the east and Belfast in the west. The southern part of the island is across from Lincolnville to the west and across from Great Spruce Head and North Haven on the east. Islesboro divides the waters that surround it into East and West Penobscot Bay and its axis runs northeast/southwest.

During the Revolutionary War, some of the old settlers traded with the British garrisoned in Castine. Castine is just a short sail away from the northern part of the island and the British were eager to buy food from locals. Loyalists in Castine were not as neighborly as the British. They often raided island homes. Generally, the old settlers of Islesboro just tried to sell what they produced and hoped that neither side in the conflict would find them offensive.

The last and largest of the tall ships built on Islesboro

was the brig *Melissa*, launched in 1837, twenty-four years before the start of the Civil War. The end of shipbuilding did not mean a decline in the island's prosperity, however. In 1850, the population of the island was nine hundred and eighty-four and in 1860, the population was twelve hundred and seventy-six. The nearly 30 percent increase in ten years means that the Islesboro economy was growing and attracting people to the island. It was during these years that the population of the island reached a number that it has not matched since.

Shipping continued to create island fortunes even after the *Melissa* was launched. *The History of Islesborough*, published in 1893 by Joseph P. Farrow, lists sixty-nine Islesboro captains and their vessels in the 1840s. One Islesboro native whose fortune was made in shipping during that time was Captain Walter F. Dodge, born April 11, 1816. He owned the *Rialto*, a schooner built on Islesboro. Of Captain Dodge, Farrow wrote:

He was a merchant, and largely interested in commerce... Capt. Dodge took charge of one of the coasting vessels early in life, when he amassed considerable property, owning in a large number of the coasting vessel. He left off going to sea and went into trade... At the age of 35 [in 1851] he was one of the wealthiest men on Islesborough. Towards the last of his life he moved to Boston, but returned to Islesborough, where he died, Aug. 16, 1869.

Shipping and mercantilism must have been popular careers but so was fishing.

Captain Joseph Collins, born on the island on August 8, 1839, devoted his life to the American fisheries. Farrow wrote:

His boyhood days were spent as a fisher lad, going boat-fishing with his grandfather before he was nine years old. His tenth birthday was spent at sea aboard a fishing schooner. In 1862, when only twenty-three years old, young Collins was appointed command of a fishing vessel, and has since commanded some of the finest schooners engaged in the fishing business from Gloucester, Mass., most of the time being at sea the whole of each year.

Captain Collins served many years on the United States Fish Commission, suggested improvements in the design of fishing vessels, and prepared exhibitions promoting the American fisheries at international fairs. He is not mentioned in Farrow's list of Islesboro men who enlisted, who were drafted, who served as substitutes, or who paid the commutation fee. Since he was the captain of a Gloucester fishing schooner in 1862, he may have moved off of the island before the Civil War began. But Collins is an example of an Islesboro resident who prospered and made a reputation in the fisheries around the time of the story of Wesley and Sabrina Brown.

As might be expected, there was some farming on the island as well. Potatoes seem to have been a cash crop beginning in the early 1800s. Farrow wrote that potatoes were shipped to Boston, so enough were grown to feed Islesboro residents and sell the surplus for income. In 1816, potatoes were the only vegetable that grew on the island, and even then only in sheltered areas, because the summer was so cold. On July 5, water froze to the thickness of glass. None of the warmer months was without frost on at least some days. Farrow's history records severely low temperatures and heavy snows throughout the first seventy or so years of the nineteenth century. Some climatologists have attributed such persistent cold to a Little Ice Age.

The third mention of potatoes on Islesboro is in 1845, when Sabrina was five years old. Farrow recorded, "A total failure of the potato crop, on account of the potato rot." This was Islesboro's experience with the same potato blight that struck Ireland during the 1840s. That blight sent Irish streaming to the States to find relief from the famine that followed the failure of the Irish potato crop. Many Irish landed in Boston and then settled in the Lewiston and Auburn area, where they were employed building the mills that Wesley described in his letter to Sabrina dated April 1860.

It must have been because the potato was a staple of agriculture on the island that Farrow includes a fourth reference to the tuber. In 1874, the "Colorado beetle (potato bug) made its first appearance." The record of the first appearance of the beetle has the tone of an ominous threat to the island potato crop.

The trades thrive in regions where the population is growing steadily. So a person employed in any trades typical of the period would have enjoyed steady employment on Islesboro: smiths and wrights of all types, mariners who were not owners of their own ships, and young woodworkers like Wesley Brown, who was optimistic that with his skills and tools he could build a home and support Sabrina well enough so she wouldn't have to work.

# SABRINA SEELEY

Sabrina, born on Islesboro on May 24, 1840, was the third child of Captain John Seeley and his island wife, Phebe Veazie. She had two older brothers: Robert and Charles, a younger brother, Mighill, and a sister, Lucinda—nicknamed Luky—who was the youngest of the five siblings. All were born on Islesboro. The record of the Seeley family in the *History of Islesborough* is very short because John Seeley came to the island from some other place, perhaps Groton, Connecticut. The Veazie family had lived on the island for fifty-five years before Sabrina was born.

John and Phebe married in 1834 and had their first child, Robert Nelson, in 1835. Sabrina was born five years later, in 1840. Phebe died in 1849, when Sabrina was nine years old and Luky was five. It was after Phebe's death that John moved the family to Groton, Connecticut, where he married Cornelia Niles.

In December 1855, when Sabrina was fifteen, her older brother Charles, seventeen, was lost at sea en route to Liverpool on the schooner *Sophie Collins*. According to notes written by Alice Pendleton (Sabrina's daughter), Charles "fell from aloft." Since Charles did not fall onto the deck, where his body could have been recovered, he might have slipped off of the rigging as the schooner pitched and rolled in a heavy sea. In December, ice might have been a problem for a sailor aloft. Charles probably fell as the rigging on which he was standing was suspended above the water, not above the deck. Included in Alice's notes is a poem written by Mighill Seeley—then ten years old—in memory of his older brother:

> Charley is dead and buried in the deep
> Where he cannot hear the little birds peep
> Where the vast waters above him roll.
> Charley poor Charley
> Peace to thy soul!

Ten months later, the sea struck again. Here is the story of that tragedy from the *New York Herald*, November 28, 1856:

LOSS OF THE SCHOONER SPLENDID—CREW SUPPOSED TO HAVE PERISHED.
Hyannis, Oct. 27, 1856
The steamer *Massachusetts* went on Saturday to the schooner reported ashore on Tuckernuck [Nantucket]. She had gone to pieces, and the crew was supposed to have perished. On the stern was the name "Splendid", of New London. Mr. S.C. Bishop, telegraph operator, found on Muskeag a trunk containing cloths, letters, &c., belonging to Capt. John Seeley, of schooner Splendid, of New London which are in the hands of the Collector of Nantucket, subject to the order of the friends of Capt. Seeley; also in the trunk, were the certificates of membership of the Masonic Lodge, which are in the hands of the Order at Nantucket. Mr. Bishop has given orders for his men to make a thorough search on the shore for the bodies of the crew.

In her notes, Alice Pendleton wrote that only the captain's body was recovered. Captain Seeley's body is buried in the Groton Cemetery, also called the Colonel Leyard Cemetery, in Groton, Connecticut. In a letter written to Alice Pendleton and dated January 1934, Merton Chapman, the sexton of the cemetery, doubted if anyone other than Captain Seeley is buried there because of the location of the monument in the plot. The inscription on the stone reads, "The body of Capt. John Seeley AE 42 rests here who with his wife Cordelia AE 36 and Son Mighill AE 14 drowned Oct. 23 – 1856." The wording of the inscription supports the sexton's suspicion that only one body lies there. Though the captain, Cordelia, and Mighill all drowned in the same tragedy, only the captain's body was recovered and buried in Groton.

A fragment of a letter from a shipping agent reveals the process of how people learn about untimely deaths. The letter is particularly poignant because it was written to Cordelia after she died but the agent did not know that he was writing to someone who would not respond. He would discover his innocent mistake soon enough. Until then, he would wonder what happened to the captain and schooner that shipped a load of Pennsylvania coal and was not heard from within a reasonable period of time. The agent wrote:

*On the 10$^{th}$ of October I rec.d from the Penn Coal Co. New York a Bill of Lading of Coal shipped by the above Company per Schooner Splendid and signed by John Seeley as Master.*

*Since the above mentioned date I have learned nothing from the vessel or the master and learning that you were the wife of Capt. John Seeley I have taken the liberty of addressing you for the purpose of ascertaining from you if anything had come to your knowledge with reference to Mr. Seeley on the vessel.*

*On the reception of this line you will confer a great favor by giving me by return of mail what information may have come into your possession.*
*Very respectfully yours,*
*William T. Richardson*

In the letters of the collection, Sabrina makes no mention of the death of her parents and younger brother. Richardson's letter is the only document that comes out of the days following the tragedy and even it doesn't suggest that the worst had happened to the *Splendid*. This letter is an example of how irony is not a contrived or artificial literary device, but that it is a living and powerful vehicle for the transmission of feelings, in this case removing the passage of more than a century of time and affecting us as if we were reading this letter as Sabrina herself was reading it, moments after taking the letter out of its envelope. The letter moves us even now to imagine and feel how Sabrina felt while reading it, knowing all along that its recipient—her stepmother—was dead and knowing that the blameless writer, Mr. Richardson, was assuming that he was making a reasonable request for information from someone who was alive. We don't miss reading Sabrina's reflections on the death of her parents and younger brother—if they ever existed—when the irony that envelops Richardson's letter affects us so profoundly. The tragedy orphaned Captain John Seeley's three remaining children: Robert, Sabrina, and Lucinda.

It is very likely that Robert was at sea when his father died. Instead of living without parents or with their older, surviving brother, Sabrina and Luky moved back to Islesboro.

*The house where Captain John Seeley, his wife Phebe, and daughters Sabrina and Lucinda lived is circled and labled "Capt. J Veazie" in this segment of the 1850 Waldo County census map. The house is presently owned by Raymond Lillie. Photo by Randy Purinton.*

The 1860 federal census records that they boarded with their uncle, Captain James Veazie, who owned a house on the northeastern part of the island, on the side of a gentle hill that overlooked Castine, Hutchins Island, and Cape Rosier. According to Alice Pendleton, it was the same house where the girls' parents—Captain John Seeley and Phebe Veazie—lived. During Sabrina's time there, in the mid-nineteenth century, a mature apple tree grew in the full sun of the front yard, just feet from the front door. That apple tree, its trunk thick and gnarled, still stands and yields apples more than good enough for pies.

*Captain James Veazie's house in Pripet, northern Islesboro, probably in the later nineteenth century. The apple tree that shades the front door still produces good fruit. Islesboro Historical Society.*

# COURTSHIP

The correspondence began on Islesboro, where Sabrina wrote her first letter. She was responding to a letter from Wesley Brown, who, at that time, was living in Auburn, Maine, single, twenty-one, and boarding with a family friend while he sought employment as a carpenter. This is the earliest letter in the collection and in it Sabrina was recalling her first conversation with her future husband. Sabrina remembered that he seemed interested in her age and finances:

*N. Islesboro Aug 23/60*
*Dear Wesley*
*I rec'd your kind epistle of the 11$^{th}$. Was much pleased to hear from you but I assure you I was in quite a dilemma to know what manner of spirit you was directed by when you thought of writing me, as I had about come to the wise conclusion that W.A. Brown had sought the far west or some distant quarter without as much as saying good by—*

*Wesley, I commenced writing this one week ago but owing to a very bad headache and several other causes, I was unable to finish it but I will endeavor to now. Have been to church all day. Saw your brother Charles there. He came from Bangor with L.P.Gilkey. What a pity it is that you was not here your birthday. You're a <u>free boy</u> now*

*Are you not Wesley. I'm not quite so yet. I shan't tell you my age Wesley although I would ask why you asked one such a question as that? And who was the author of the letter in which was insinuated that you was after my money, in lieu of Brina. A very profitable exchange*

I should think. I will say in regard to that question. It would be impossible for me to give you any answer if I wished to as I know not how much I am the possessor of. My guardian always transacted all my business matters when I was at home and since I came here I have seldom troubled myself to inquire in to the state of my affairs and I placed full confidence in his fidelity, sending me a check when I required it. I am not of age to take any thing in my own name therefore, friend W. you perceive I'm not much in business matters, but I expect before many years to call the "master of the vineyard such to give an account of his \_\_\_\_\_ and ships". Perhaps at that period Wesley if I should happen to share in your acquaintance, I might give you a more correct answer.

You asked where brother [Robert Nelson] was now. I expect he is in Barbados at present. From there he thought of going to Europe, so he wrote me from Port Medway "only over the waters I think I shall tire of looking for the Jeffrey ere I see her." O Wesley was you aware that I was indebted to you the sum of 7 cts? Well, I am. You sent a [foring] stamp for brother's letter and he was in N. York so I mailed your letter and sent your stamp to Port May on a letter of mine. Quite convenient wasn't it Wesley, for <u>me.</u> Harry is not at home now. A letter came to him from you, and Elija requested me to say to you that you "need not fear to come." What does she mean? Are you coming to the Island soon, please to tell me, that is a <u>good boy.</u> ... I may see you sometime, and if I never do why that will help me remember you, Wesley.

You said that you would like one of my presents. You are welcome to half a dozen if you wish. But I must close and stop tracking this paper. So a pleasant Sabbath

*with you.*
    *S P Seeley*

When Sabrina mentioned that she saw Wesley's brother, Charles Buckley Brown (later to be the builder of the first Islesboro Inn), at the church, she probably saw him at the Freewill Baptist Church built in 1843 on the northern part of the island. Sabrina's grandfather John Veazie reserved a pew in that church, as did her uncle John Veazie Jr., who was still alive when Sabrina and Luky returned to Islesboro from Groton. So it's likely that Sabrina was sitting in John Jr.'s pew when Charles B. Brown and his friend Lycurgus P. Gilkey entered.

There are no letters extant from the months between August and March. But during that time Wesley introduced Sabrina to some members of his family. Wesley's sister Minta liked Sabrina and told him that she looked forward to the day when she could call Sabrina her sister.

*East Auburn March 29/60*
*Dear Friend S,*
*It is with pleasure that I now pen a few lines to you to inform you of my safe arrival in this place, also of my good health, and that of my Brother's family. But I must begin by asking you to excuse this very poor writing for I have not a single pen fit to write with, and being a poor writer, it makes bad work—Perhaps an account of my trip to this place might interest you, hoping it will I will endeavor to give it. I (as you know) started from Islesboro March 26th, stopped in Belfast that night and until the next PM then took the stage for Bangor. While riding in the stage formed the acquaintance of Mrs. Winslow, teacher*

*of the "select school of Belfast," who was going out of town to spend her vacation, enjoyed myself quite well until she stopped and then it was dull enough I assure you. We arrived at Bangor at 10 P.M. just as we were going into the City, the Bells pealed an alarm of fire, and so instead of riding...and did not retire until 2 o'clock A.M. spent the next day and evening visiting my friends in B. Next A.M. took the morning train for Lewiston where I arrived safe, and well the same P.M. Went to Minta's but found no one with whom I was acquainted Chas being at Lewiston to work and Minta having gone and visit. She came today, sends much love to her "hope-she-will-be-sister" Brina—Dear Sabrina if you deem this worthy an answer write soon, write all the news you can think of. And dearest write a long letter for one word from you would influence me more than <u>all else.</u> I expect to work here for a short time but do not think that I shall go to California very soon. Do not let Lucinda see this, but burn it as soon as you get it (<u>won't you</u>) for it is written so poorly that I am ashamed of it and it is my especial request that you burn it, and say so when you write and next time I will try and do better. Dearest, may you be happy as you deserve to be which in my opinion would be as happy as Mortal can be ever will be the prayer of your sincere and devoted Friend Wesley A. Brown. Be sure and burn this before you write. Don't write until you do. Yours Truly, W.P.S. Be very careful and not expose yourself and learn French as fast as you please. My love to Lucinda, respects to Mr. Veazie and [Leadlz] and much love to "Brina". Please excuse this scrawl. Write soon.*

  *W.A. Brown*

Wesley was a modest young man. Though he criticized his own writing skills, he was at least as skilled as an average twenty-something today. Yet he judged his writing to be so inferior that he insisted that Sabrina burn his letter so as not to be embarrassed if Sabrina's sister, Luky, read it, but Sabrina saved the letter regardless.

As we have seen, Sabrina was less inclined to burn letters than Wesley, who had to reserve space in his backpack. She believed that a person's letter was an extension of him- or herself and that a letter was vested with a life of its own. That is why she considered Wesley's letters sacred. To Sabrina and Wesley, letters were life and love.

A letter from a loved one is proof to a soldier that he is remembered and loved regardless of his obligation to kill. Besides being a means to carry supplies, a canvas backpack was like a sanctum; letters were reminders of a soldier's humanity and having to destroy those reminders to create space in a backpack was regrettable. But worst of all, letters tossed and scattered on a recent battlefield confirmed that a sanctum had been breached and somewhere there was blood on the ground.

Sabrina seems to have been well educated and maybe that made Wesley feel like her intellectual inferior. By island standards, Sabrina was educated well enough to be a certified teacher. Days before Wesley enlisted and left the island, Sabrina received her teaching certificate, which reads:

State of Maine

Waldo S.S. [Superintendent of Schools]

This certifies that in the opinion of the undersigned Mrs. Sabrina Brown sustains a good moral character; and possess a temper and disposition suitable for teacher of youth; that she is qualified to govern and discipline a school, and to instruct in Reading, Spelling, Writing, English Grammar, Geography, History, Arithmetic and such other branches of learning as are usually taught in public schools, and particularly in those branches required in Dist. 6 in the town of Islesboro.

Thomas G. Moody
William P. Boardman, Superintending School Committee Islesboro April 22$^{nd}$ 1861

In 1847, seventeen years before there were Normal Schools—teachers' colleges—in Maine, the state created a system of teaching institutes. Sabrina was certified before the Normal Schools were established in 1867, so she might have graduated from one of these institutes or the island school committee might have granted her certificate based on a strong academic record she achieved while living in Connecticut, island contacts, and a good interview. For a short time, Sabrina taught in District 6 in the northern part of the island. This district was called the Sprague or West District. There was a school just a short distance north of Rathburn D. Sprague's house on the west side of the island, across the road from Greenwood Cemetery. Sabrina's letters reveal no discussion of her activities as an island teacher.

Sabrina's language skills were very good. She read the newspapers and the Bible and she appreciated art. Her education might have been directed and encouraged by both her birth mother, Phebe, and, later, her stepmother, Cordelia.

It might be that the Veazie family thought it would

be most appropriate for them to take in the orphaned daughters of Phebe, thus bringing the sisters back to Islesboro after an absence of some years. So this means that for a few years after Sabrina's tenth birthday, Cordelia, and maybe to some extent the Veazie family, was responsible for educating the young woman that Sabrina would become. It may be that Cordelia was the source of Sabrina's appreciation of learning and the arts. Cordelia might have taught Brina how to sew and knit, as well. Maybe Cordelia herself was a teacher.

The tone of Wesley's letter brightened when he told Brina about having met Mrs. Winslow on the stage. Wesley missed the teacher's company like he missed the company of his scholarly Brina.

Wesley's first letter from Auburn began a flurry of letters—the collection is missing one or two from Brina during this time—in which Wesley proposes, in a general way. He asks Brina if she could imagine herself as his wife. He desperately wants to marry her but can't script an outright and unambiguous proposal. As a prelude to a process that Wesley believed he must follow, he first expressed his loneliness and his passion. Then, he wanted to know if everything that had happened between them so far was satisfactory to Brina. He is honest about his prospects of finding work as a carpenter and he revealed his financial debt. Finally, he confessed that Brina was his one love and that she would always be so. Wesley took a risk and he had to wait for Brina's response. By combining the letters Wesley sent on April 8 and April 16, Wesley's proposal emerges from a text that includes a variety of reflections related to his life as a young, transient, single carpenter searching for work in a region of Maine that was undergoing rapid industrialization:

*Dearest Friend: Tis a beautiful Sabbath morning way up here in Auburn. The sun shines out warm and clear, the fields begin to look green and everything seems to say that stern old man winter's reign is about past. But for all that I am lonesome and would like to know how my best loved friend Brina is feeling this morning, does she find anything to interest her or is she too lonesome, is her health good and has she learned French yet... I have been away from the Island hardly two weeks and yet it seems very long. During that time I have read and reread all the letters I ever had from you, at least a dozen times, having worn out a certain daguerreotype case which contains your likeness...*

*Yours of the 8th was duly received on the 11th and was read with great pleasure by me. I am very sorry that Lucinda is so sick, and hope by your next [letter] to hear that she is better, tell her I had no chance in Bangor to send her those Spanish books that I spoke to her of. I was very much interested in your minute description of that "Speaking School" for which accept my sincere thanks. Your account of [the] "Slay Ride" was very much as the real... Lewiston is pleasantly situated on the east side of the Androscoggin river, it is a very growing place and will eventually be The Place of this state. The companies that own the chief part of the land are continually filling up the valleys, demolishing hills, building factories where there was nothing but a forest of trees four years ago there is now factories worth millions of dollars. The Hill Company who own some land there are going to expand on factories the present year $1,000,000 besides some other buildings...*

*Dam, mill and railroad in Lewiston, Maine: products of mid-nineteenth century industrialization.*

From John S.C. Abbot's THE HISTORY OF MAINE, published in 1875. Photo by Randy Purinton.

*This forenoon was up to Turner about six miles from here from whence I could see several peaks of the White Mountains, Mts. Washington and Jefferson being of the number. On account of the atmosphere being in a peculiar mood the mountains did not appear to be more than twenty miles distant but in reality they were nearer one hundred and yet this all may not interest you and so I will stop it...*

*Dear Friend I feel that tis my duty (being such friends that we are, I hope) to inform you of my prospects, so that you may do nothing which you may afterwards regret. I am now without work as I have since my arrival here but hope soon to be able to get some of some kind... My object in writing this is that I sometimes fear that you may regret what has passed between us and wish it "annulled". If so it is within your power to do it, but Dear Girl, I had rather hear of the death of my best friend that you should do so. Mine, Sabrina, is a nature that loves but once, and that love is centered in you. I may at times appear odd, sometimes in your company I may have appeared even cold, and distant, yet twas not because I did not feel, it was for the reason mentioned a few lines back, knowing that you have had more time to think of these things in my absence, I anxiously wait a reply to this. Meanwhile and always I will subscribe myself your True and loving Friend Wesley.*

The wait began. A letter or two arrived that were mailed before Wesley's letter of inquiry and so they didn't relieve the wait, but those letters were not as important as the one that has survived: the one dated April 24, in which Sabrina used language that suggested a marriage vow was being made. Poetry is included, local news was shared, and Sabrina even included a little French. How this letter survived and the others were lost or burned is a mystery. Either Wesley intentionally left it at home before he went off to war or Sabrina found a safe place for it:

*This 24$^{th}$ of April is very beautiful and pleasant. The sunshine is warm and just air enough to call it one of spring's most lovely days. Thought I would not improve an hour better than in penning you a few lines in answer to yours of the 16$^{th}$ in which I read with pleasure and was much interested in your account of Lewiston and its flourishing state. I should like to have been with you when you saw Mts. Washington and Jefferson for I dearly love the mountains so grand and high with their snow-capped peaks that seem to touch the sky. I think them one of nature's most sublime perfections...*

*Dear Wesley, now in regard to what you wrote last referring to yourself. I was very sorry that you were without work, for time must hang rather heavy on your hands. I fancy you misjudge me if you think that I would wish annulled what has passed between us. No, Wesley, I do not wish it and it would take more than anything so transient as money to cause me to wish otherwise. I have took pleasure in your society, been happy in thinking you my friend, and know of no other person in whose welfare I interest. You call me friend. I would myself such, not only in prosperity but when the cold winds of adversity blanch and should cause the heart to turn in sorrow from [loving] charms. It is then, dear Wesley, you will find Brina the same. You won't be discouraged* when life may look gloomy now. There is sunshine in store for you yet.

>  *Be cheerful and happy*
>  *Have joy while you may*
>  *Life cannot last always*
>  *It hasteth away.*

Luky is better so she can go outdoors a short distance—she had forgotten the books entirely—there are quite enough here now. Capt. Benjamin Warren was here today. Mrs. Edgar Hatch was buried today. Mrs. Emiline Hatch is a raving maniac. Threw a cup of gruel in Rev. Burbanks face came near putting his eye out—tore his hair off of him, etc. they have put her in a straight jacket. Miss Mary Dodge down the island is to be buried tomorrow. Edgar Bunker I understand broke his leg driving an ugly pair of steers—broke it very badly, which is worse, poor fellow. They say Mary Ann Dodge has got a beau. She never was going to get married; perhaps she won't as there is many a slip between the cup and lip. Charley Morris passed here last Sabbath. I shall soon close my tracking for Brina don't feel very well this afternoon. Please excuse this commonplace letter and give my best respects to all enquiring friends and many wishes for your welfare. I will subscribe myself as your affectionate friend,
  Brina Seeley
Response s'il vous plait.

>  *In pleasure's dreams and sorrow's hour*
>  *In crowded hall or lonely bower*
>  *The object of my life shall be*
>  *Always to remember thee.*

The colloquialism about the cup and lip is a way of

saying that what people say will happen will often be different than what does happen. The lip is a reference to what is said or spread around, as through gossip. The contents of the cup are what actually happen. If the contents are drunk then something that was talked about—"lipped about"—has actually happened. The slip between the cup and the lip is the possibility that what was talked about might not happen; for example, Mary Ann Dodge has a beau but she might not get married, even if people are speculating that she will. Even today, much time is devoted to speculating about what others will do.

Sabrina's closing poem is a reminder that, as promised, she did take upon herself the responsibility to always remember Wesley and she did that by storing the correspondence in a trunk. More history of their marriage was created by letters than by the words spoken between husband and wife while they lived that one month in each other's company. In Sabrina's case, when she spoke of preserving Wesley's memory, she did drink of the cup and fulfilled the promise written in her poem, "Always to remember thee."

Wesley was thrilled by the content of Sabrina's latest letter:

*East Auburn April 2-1860*
*Dearly Beloved Friend*
*I had begun to think it almost impossible for one as gifted with such a mind as you have to care for me, a homeless, penniless and not over-gifted wanderer but your very kind letter dispelled all my doubts as I know you*

*are not one to profess what you do not feel. I am, as yet, out of employment which no doubt tended to make me more distrustful of you, my best, beloved Brina for which, dearest, you must forgive me. Would that my prospects were better, yet not being so, I suppose it is as Brina says, "All for the best."*

*I was glad to hear that Luky was better, give her my love, and tell her that "Brother Wes" wants her to get well, as quick as she possibly can, so as to send him a May Flower, in your next, of her own picking. Dear Sabrina, in your care of Luky, and the attendant wearing of such a care, do not, I beg, forget that you aren't constitutionally as strong as many and do not overtask yourself, for remember that you are beloved by many to whom without your dear company life would have few attractions and those of an ordinary kind.*

*But dear S, with you as friend and with the reward some time not far hence that I hope to claim from your hand, "Excelsior" shall be my motto and in my vocabulary there shall be no such word as Fail...be assured that I shall ever remember last evening [upon reading your letter] as one of the Sunshiny spots in my checkered life—*

"Excelsior" is a Latin word which means "ever higher." In 1841, the American poet Henry Wadsworth Longfellow wrote a poem using the word as its theme and title. The poem describes a young stranger who carries a banner with the word emblazoned on it. The youth carries the banner through an Alpine town driven, we think, by his determination to either cross a mountain pass locked in snow or to ascend a local mountain peak. Both an old man and a peasant try to restrain the youth by warning him of the dangers ahead. A maid offers her bosom as a resting place, hoping she can persuade the youth to accept an alternative to certain death on the mountain. But the youth won't be deterred from his errand. "Excelsior!" is his response to warnings and temptation. A St. Bernard finds the youth's frozen corpse the following morning while Heaven sighs a eulogy, "Excelsior!"

The poem was very popular during the twenty years that preceded Wesley's use of the word in his letter to Sabrina. The youth in the poem has neither goal nor destination and though wise voices warn him of lethal risks ahead, he is so driven by the pursuit that he is powerless to save himself. It's tragic. The theme seems to resonate within the American soul, a soul that is charged with nervous and sometimes reckless energy and seems addicted to moving for the sake of moving. Without a doubt, Wesley heard the poem recited by others or read the poem in a school text. Wesley chose "Excelsior" to describe his relentless quest for Sabrina's hand in marriage:

*Sabrina, a thousand thanks for that kiss which is only one of many you owe me as I have many times kissed your likeness, almost deluding myself with the belief that it was yourself, until my lips came in contact with the glass, when all delusions vanished and I could see only the facsimile of Brina, not like herself returning a kiss, but always cold, stern and inanimate. I shall send you my Daguerreotype in June if I get one taken to suit me before that time. I have had two taken but they are not good so I shall not send either of them. Chas. Will come down in June. No more until I hear from you again, Wesley*

*PS I have just returned from Turner from which place*

*one can see the White Mts very plainly. What makes them objects of interest is that they are at all times of the year covered with snow which, in a sultry August day must indeed look singular. I enjoy myself very well here. Fred Allen (my host) does everything in his power to make my stay agreeable. He has a splendid library which he placed at my disposal as soon as I arrived here. He is a very learned scholar, one that looks into the Why's and wherefores of a thing. He just entered the room where I am and says, "Tell Sabrina that if she will come up here I will get her an easy school to teach and then Wes you will be more contented." I should add my earnest entreaties to the above did I think it would be of any avail—Fred says, "Sabrina may have one of my kittens if she will come and get it." They are his pets her being an old Bach, but he is about to be married and I suppose he thinks that his wife will be jealous if he keeps them all. But goodnight and pleasant dreams to Brina—Wesley*

Wesley was a witness to the last years of the Little Ice Age, a period of colder weather around the globe between the fourteenth and mid-nineteenth centuries. Wesley told Sabrina that there was snow on the White Mountains year-round and that he saw snow on the peaks even during a sultry day in August. Though it does snow every month of the year on Mt. Washington, what Wesley saw was the last evidence of a snow-pack that endured for centuries and which gave the White Mountains its name. The Little Ice Age ended around 1850, when the glaciers and snow fields formed during that period began melting. No person alive today can claim that he has seen snow on the peaks of the White Mountains from one hundred miles away on a sultry day in August, and no person in this century and probably the next will see what Wesley saw.

Though Wesley swears he will not write another word before he receives a letter from Brina, he added a postscript so long that we know that he couldn't restrain himself despite what he vowed. He had to kiss Sabrina's image and he had to write to her.

In Wesley's last letter in this series, he revels in the idea that he will be Sabrina's husband. He also admits to having written about the White Mountains in a previous letter and apologizes. But of interest in this letter is the mention of a patriotic lecture titled "Our Washington" that he heard delivered by a popular speaker, the Honorable Edward Everett, a former U.S. representative and U.S. senator, former governor of Massachusetts, and president of Harvard College. Everett delivered this speech across America, in both Northern and Southern states, hoping that Americans would remain united as a country if they could be persuaded that they shared in common an almost mythic hero in the person of their first president. In addition to appealing to their national spirit, Everett raised one hundred thousand dollars to purchase Mt. Vernon, Washington's estate and burial place, now a national shrine. Wesley's reaction to the speech is evidence that he could be moved by patriotic themes, just like he could be moved by the spirit of "Excelsior." He heard Everett speak on Tuesday, April 24, 1860. According to Sabrina's diary, Wesley made the decision to enlist sometime between April 24 and 25, 1861, exactly one year later.

Exactly a year separated Wesley's death on September 23, 1862, from the two-hour oration that Everett delivered on

September 23, 1863, during the dedication of the national cemetery at Gettysburg. Fortunately, it wasn't as hot on the field that day compared to the first three days of July of that same year, when the Battle of Gettysburg was fought. Everett's oration was well received but Lincoln's address, lasting about two minutes, said pretty much what Everett said, though with a stunning economy of words. Lincoln's address is revered, whereas Everett's address is not. Sadly, Everett did not live to celebrate the end of the war. He died at age sixty-nine, three months before Lee's surrender at Appomattox, on April 9, 1865. Lincoln was assassinated five days after the war ended, at age fifty-six. In April, 1860, five years earlier, Wesley was living in Lewiston, Maine:

*Lewiston Apr 29/60*
*Ever dear Friend*
*It is with pleasure that I now take pen in hand to attempt to answer your kind letter of the 24$^{th}$ which assured me of your unchanged affection for which I am very thankful. My health is not very good at present as I have not spoke aloud for nearly a week having a very bad cold, but the prospect is good, at present, for a recovery without anything serious—You will see by the date of this letter that I am in Lewiston, at present. I came here last week having found employment for a short time. My address is still the same as it has been—Brina I had the pleasure of hearing the Hon Edward Everett last Tuesday eve, his subject was that never failing ever interesting theme "Our Washington" and I think if justice was ever done to the memory of that great and good man by oratory it was by Everett on that evening. His mighty mind seemed to be*

*fully able to accomplish the great task he had undertaken so that the hearer saw Washington in his true light as a man in the highest sense of the word. Dear S, if my prospects were better I should wish that we might be married this fall (don't blush) if you would consent to it, but as I am situated it would be folly for me to ask it of you, as I have no home to take you to, nor will your health permit of the labor housekeeping, were it so that it could be we might be very happy, at least I should be with you always near me, but that might not be agreeable with you, would it. Say, did you ever think of having Wesley for a husband. Do you think that he would be a good one. Do you think that he could earn enough to support Brina as she should be so that she would not be obliged to work. Answer all of the above and oblige him. I am sure that he would do all he could if Brina would consent to it but it would be asking too much—*

*In that which I wrote last Sabbath I see that I spoke of something which by reading your last I suppose I have written of before. You will excuse this poor writing from your friend. Be very careful of your health and do not get sick for you have no older sister to watch over you. If I have written anything foolish in here overlook it—*

*See what a long letter a whole sheet of foolishness while yours are very short. As soon as you get this seat yourself and write one twice as long—my love to all and most of it to Brina. Wesley—*

So in their own way, in April 1860, through their correspondence, Wesley and Sabrina agreed to marry. Wesley suggested a ceremony in the fall but they would marry the following March, in 1861.

*A lock of Wesley's mother's hair. The note is in Wesley's handwriting. Islesboro Historical Society.*

# MOTHER

At least a year before Wesley's search for employment in Auburn and Lewiston, Wesley's mother, Sarah, moved west from Maine to Monticello, Wisconsin, with her second husband—Wesley's paternal father, John Brown, having died in 1839. A daughter, Mary—Wesley's younger sister—accompanied her, and Wesley seems to have had a younger brother, Hiram, too. Wesley's mother missed her children Wesley and George terribly, and truthfully didn't know if she would ever see them again. A lock of her hair is preserved in a folded piece of paper among the letters of the correspondence, probably sent by her to Wesley and George as a way of being physically present in their lives despite the distance that separated them.

She was a pious woman whose advice to her son Wesley included admonitions to lead a virtuous life. She talked about being ailing and overworked with eyesight so poor that it was difficult to write letters longer than a page, but she did write as often as she could and she loved all of her children very much. In a letter to Wesley dated May 1859, her piety and her concern for her son's physical as well as moral well-being were evident:

*Monticello May 12, 1859*
*My Dear Son*
*I need hardly tell you how glad I was to receive a letter from you but my heart was pained when I heard of your lame back don't lift any thing that is heavy tell the man that you work for that you will work for less wages if you will take a wet cloth and bind around your back*

*every night and then put a flannel over that it will help you I think do try it my dear child and see if it will not do you some good how I wish you were here to have a Mothers care your Father is so homesick that I don't know but he will go to Maine this fall it is hard telling what he will do I wish it was in my power to help you but it is not so I the time will soon come that I can see your face in the land of the living may God bless you my dear one with much of his grace I want you to go to meeting and not be with them that profane God's holy day shun the wicked and profane honor God and you will never be sorry when you are tempted to sin think of your dead father how it would grieve him to see you led into sin and O my son it would bring me sorrow to the grave you are young and need much wisdom to guard you from the many snares that are set for young men in the cities I want you to write and let me know how much you get a month and who you work for be very careful of your health you will be more like to have a fever again than you would if you never had been sick Bangor is very unhealthy in the summer and I shall feel anxious all the time about you don't expose yourself to the night air it is very bad write as often as you can may God bless you my son your affectionate Mother Henry has gone to Broadhead green Co*

Mary added to the letter by saying:

*Dear Brother Wesley It has been a long time since I herd from you It is Sunday today & I have wrote Three letters this afternoon I went to meeting this forenoon & heard a Methodist man preach I should like to see you Very much We had a letter from Hiram a week ago to*

*day our school commences tomoro I wish that you would come out West & teach school next Winter Mother got a letter from you just a week ago to day the next Time you write to Mother write a few lines to me Hiram says that SF is very pleasant he said that the Hills looked like one vast flour Garden I should think It would look Very Beautiful I think flowrs Are Very Beautiful I cannot think of any more to Write So good by*
    *from,*
    *Mary*

Young Mary's love of beauty and flowers contrasts with the bleak tone of Mother's letter. It must have been a challenge for the girl to live with such gloomy parents, missing her adventurous older brothers, suggesting that Wesley could find employment as a teacher if he moved to Wisconsin. The poor girl was trapped in a house of chronic fatigue and homesickness.

Late in 1860, Wesley told his mother about his and Sabrina's intention to marry. It must have lifted his mother's heart when Wesley wrote to her asking for advice concerning marriage. It was the kind of familial contact that was missing in her life after her move west. Her response to Wesley's request, dated November 11, 1860, was brief and took the form of an invitation to bring his future bride for a visit:

*My Dear Son: I received a letter from you asking my advice about getting married. I hardly know what to say if I was where you are I could tell better I think you could get work here if you wanted to what do you think about getting married and coming out here on a bridal tour and taking your chest of tools along with you I think you could get work here let your wife stay with me and make me a visit I would not want to advize you any thing that would not be in your interest I hope my dear child that you will consider well what you are doing and ask God to direct you. I hope that Sabrina is as good as you say. If she is she is none too good for my oldest baby I should like to see you all very much May God bless you my dear children I have been sick and cannot write but little. Your mother.*

A letter dated May 1, 1861, was written five days after Wesley left Sabrina and Islesboro forever. Because it would have taken more than three or four days for a letter from Maine to reach Wisconsin, she couldn't have known that Wesley had enlisted and was by then in Belfast with other Union volunteers. The tone of Wesley's mother's letters is often gloomy. She was a fatalist—a pious fatalist. Though she did not know Wesley was in the army at the time of her writing, her fatalistic outlook on life makes the letter read like a premonition of death:

*Monticello May 1, 1861*
*My dear Son I wrote you a letter and have been waiting a long time for an answer I am afraid you are sick how I wish I could send you money to come out here with [Sabrina] do write me as often as you can and let me know all your joys and sorrows my health is quite poor I have the spinal affection I hope that you will be careful of your health I have worked so hard since your Father died that my health is all broken down O Wesley you lost a good*

*Father he thought every thing of his children I expect it would have been better for you if your father had lived and I had been taken away I hope that God will indeed be a father to you my dear son and bless you with much of his grace I hope that your aim will be to do good to be a good man and the blessing of God will rest on you I hope that we shall see each other again in the flesh but if not may we meet in heaven where there will be no more parting give much love to Charles & wife accept a large share yourself love to all inquiring friends your Affectionate Mother*

If Wesley did consider a visit west with Sabrina, the advent of the war and his enlistment a month after his wedding ended any such dream. Sarah died in 1865, knowing her son would welcome her in Paradise.

## SABRINA SEELEY BROWN

Now it is March 28, 1861, the day of Wesley and Sabrina's wedding that took place on Islesboro, Maine, maybe in the Veazie house, where Sabrina and Luky lived, or another in which the two newlyweds were to live only one month before Wesley enlisted. A local Baptist minister, Reverend James Small, a neighbor, officiated. Naturally there are no letters describing the wedding because Sabrina and Wesley were both there, but Sabrina wrote a short entry in her diary that day:

*Thursday, March 28th, 1861. Pleasant but quite windy. Wesley having me meet the witnesses of my marriage which I expect will take place this eve. It makes me quite sober to think about it knowing that my future depends on him I have chosen.—PM Was married about one-half of eight. Had a very pleasant time.*

Wesley kept a diary also. His entry for March 28:
*Thursday [March] 28, 1861: Very pleasant in every sense of the word it being my marriage. Invited guests this AM 35 in number three in the house making 38. Was united to Brina at 7 ½ oclock PM*

Henry Wheeler of Bangor, Wesley's cousin, would have liked to attend the wedding but he sent this letter on that day instead:

*Thursday, March 28, 1861. That is a date, dear Wesley, which will always be stamped indelibly on your mind. If the happy ceremony takes place today this will be one of* *the important days of your life. Now you have an object to live for, something more than self to care for. Although it was impossible for me to be present with you today, you have my wishes for health, peace and happiness. May your union prove to be the perfection of conjugal felicity... I want you to write to me as soon as possible after the receipt of this as I shall be dying to know <u>all the particulars</u>... What do you intend to do this summer Wesley—are you going to play "love in the cottage", hey? If you do I shall go to see you after you get settled and make the acquaintance of Mrs. B. Your affectionate cousin, Henry W. Wheeler.*

The tone of Henry's letter is light, amusing, and familiar. Henry and Wesley were as close as brothers. Indeed, Henry, Wesley, and Wesley's brother George enlisted together. Within months, Henry, the would-be wedding guest who understood the poignancy of writing a letter to his cousin on Wesley's wedding day, would be a Union soldier on the battlefield at Bull Run, volunteering to retrieve Union wounded under fire, on a hot and chaotic day in July 1861, an act of bravery for which Henry would earn the Congressional Medal of Honor.

# ENLISTMENT AND DEPARTURE

On April 12, 1861, fifteen days after vows were exchanged in what Wesley called "that little nuptial chamber" on Islesboro, Fort Sumter was bombarded. The Civil War had begun. On April 15, only forty-two days after he was inaugurated, President Lincoln called for troops from states loyal to the Union. On April 21, Cousin Henry again wrote to Wesley:

*Dear cuz: I have been anxiously awaiting a letter from you some days but have not yet received one. What is your state of mind at this time? I hope that you are willing to serve your country even to the death. I suppose you are "in arms" now, isn't it so? Two days ago a recruiting office was opened here and they have raised a company of about 75 men... I gave my employer notice yesterday... I think I shall go in the Light infantry if I can... Please write me soon for I do not know how long I shall be here. I suppose that Brina will not let you go will she... If I shouldn't have the pleasure of writing you again I will hope that kind Providence will watch over you and that your cup of happiness will be full.*

Sabrina was not party to Wesley's thoughts about the subject of enlistment but she knew in her heart that she did not want Wesley to leave her. The only evidence we have that expresses the actions and thoughts of the newly married couple in the days before Wesley's decision and several days afterwards comes from Sabrina's 1861 diary, a tiny paperback book with lined pages so small that an entry is only a few short sentences in length. What follows are the entries related to Sabrina's feelings about Wesley's departure and her realization that their marriage was going to depend on how true they would be to their correspondence:

*Wednesday April 24, 1861. At home. Wesley is on the west side and I am lonesome but I am always lonely when he is gone. Sewing, making him apron and pants. He has returned, been to the post office, received three letters wanting him to enter the service of his country. I don't want him to. It would be so lonesome at home.*

*Thursday. At home. Pleasant. Quite ill today. Wesley is at home this AM. Read to me from the life of Christ. He wrote to Henry Wheeler today. PM he went over to Pendleton's and returned. Took his [letter] from there to the [post office] thence home and informed me that he enlisted. O what sorrow there was for me. My heart seemed ready to break with that load of grief.*

*Friday. Wesley went to Castine at 2:30 this morning. O how lonely I felt. No one knows the sorrow of that hour except those that experience it.*

During these days, Wesley wrote in his diary also. The following entries record the night he left the island and the day he signed his name on a list, thereby committing himself to his country's service:

*April 25, 1861 pleasant at home...started for Castine wind blew, turned back...eve at home*

*April 26 Friday pleasant stayed at... signed the volunteer list...meeting at church great time...wrote to Brina*

*April 27 Saturday Started for Bangor...there at 8 AM eve at Charles's wrote to Brina*

*April 28 Sunday Pleasant at the barracks eve at Charles received a letter from Brina*

Wesley's first attempt to row or sail to Castine was foiled by a heavy wind so he spent the evening at home and then made a successful crossing early the morning of the April 26. We can imagine what Sabrina must have felt when Wesley returned home unexpectedly. She might have thought that he changed his mind, for instance, and for a few seconds she might have secretly been overjoyed at the thought, until Wesley explained that he would try again later. It seemed as if Fate gave Wesley one opportunity to alter what would be, and by deciding to leave for Castine the following day, Wesley himself chose a course that would make that night the last that he would spend in the company of his wife. Sabrina's diary records the stress of not knowing when, or if, she'll hear from Wesley and the thrill of receiving his first letters:

*Saturday [April 27]. Cloudy. Grandmother returned home from Searsport today. Have been looking for Wesley today and a letter but was disappointed.*

*Sunday. Cloudy. At home writing poetry. It is one month to this eve since I was married. It has been the happiest month of my checkered life. But I mustn't pine because my light is gone. It may return to shine brighter* on my life than ere before, so I will not pine at what can't be avoided.

Monday. Rain. At home PM. Making a soldier's cap for Otis Veazie. He was very much pleased with it. I am very lonely now. I don't see any letter tonight. A little disappointed but never mind, hope for the best, the worst can but come.

Tuesday. I wish I knew where my other half was tonight but I do not. May God bless and watch over him will ever be the prayer of his devoted Brina.

Wednesday. Pleasant with high winds. Mail did not go off today. At home. It's eve and I am sitting here thinking how lonesome the wind sounds. But I mustn't murmur because my lot is better than thousands of others. I mustn't look on the dark side all the time. There are always some bright spots hidden beneath the darkest gloom.

Thursday May 2, 1861 Received three letters from Wesley... I am very much pleased to hear from him. Yet up very late and wrote him eight pages.

Friday...rose at five this morning and carried Wesley's letter to the store to post in Belfast. I have just returned from the woods, having been getting syrupbarks etc. It is quite cool, wind fresh from the west.

*"I have just returned from the woods, having been getting syrup-barks etc. It is quite cool, wind fresh from the west."* Photo by Forrest G. Purinton

The cool, fresh wind from the west heralded a transition in Sabrina's life. She emerged from her desperate loneliness and gloom of the several days following her husband's departure and was again a daughter of the island who walked the rough roads to post her letters to her husband, and stalked wind-swept coastal forests and fields, foraging for medicinal barks and herbs. It sounds so primal—almost Evangelinesque—as if the island and the mail must now provide the appropriate sustenance to lead this young woman's heart out from its first disappointment.

Meanwhile, in Bangor, the Second Maine was training and making preparations to leave the state. Wesley had been writing to Sabrina faithfully and his last two letters contain details that occur only to people who know they are leaving home for awhile:

*Camp Washburn Bangor May 12th 1860*
*Dearly loved Brina*
*Again I sit down to the pleasant enjoyment of penning you a few more lines to task your patience, as this is the seventh letter I have written within the two weeks and none nor all are half as good as one of my own darling Brina's of which I have got two and for which I am very thankful and hope to read another ere I leave Bangor which I expect to do Tuesday morn at 8 A.M. I am well darling and hope that this will find you the same I will leave my clothes at Chas and get him to send them down to you so as to keep them until I get back I have left my mittens in my overcoat pocket and put my "shirt studs" in the watch pocket of my pants—*

*Do not let my tools go to anyone no matter who as I shall need them all to work with when I build FD's house this fall*

*or next spring. Take all of my things over to Pendletons and if they will board you had better stay there until I get back—If you sell your house and get the money do not invest it all at one place but put it in something that will pay and be safe but I have no need to caution my Brina for she is more competent on that score than Wesley. The word now is that we shall be paid our bounty tomorrow and if we are I will send you the most of it but part I shall have to keep to pay debts contracted here. I should like to have a revolver but I think Brina needs the money more than I do that don't you think so? Possibly I may buy one yet if the rest get one as I think I need one very much if I don't send Brina any money now would she care much under the circumstances. I believe you would approve of it if I thought she was in the least need of it I would surely send it but I cannot tell as yet what I may do. We are going either to Statten Island or Fort Monroe either of which are very healthy places but you need not send a letter until you hear from me but write a good lot and send me a "Big" package when you know where to send them as I will inform you as soon as I can. I shall buy me an India Rubber blanket when I get where they are as I believe them to be a good thing. I will write more tomorrow so now good night and may God watch over and protect you dearest and best of wives*
    *Wesley*

    *Bangor May 11$^{th}$ 1861*
*My Own Brina*
    *...Write me a little every day if convenient and send it as soon as you get a big sheet filled up and tell Luky to write real often and dearest don't expect letters from me too often as I don't expect to have much of a chance to write but will as often as I possibly can. After you get through with*

*your school and go to Conn. you can stop as long as you wish—but darling if I could see you I would cheerfully give all the pay that I shall make while I am gone but as that is not possible we must do the next best thing, i.e., write as often as we can...how do you like keeping school. Take the best care of your health. Write as often as you can and may God watch over and protect you my own dear wife. If I could see you I would kiss you a good lot.*

Wesley added to this letter the following morning. It was his last letter to Brina from Maine:

*May 13$^{th}$ Dearest we are at the barracks so busy that I cannot get a chance to go downtown so I will write a few words here we are to leave in the morning at 8 A.M. so you must excuse me for my haste. I meant to have my ambrotype taken but have no chance. Enclosed I send a couple of cousin Albert Wheelers but Henry has no chance to have his taken do not write until you hear from me they tell me that the families of the Castine Company are furnished with considerable ready money so that you will not need at present but I shall send you some if I have as chance no more this time*

*May God bless thee dearest will ever be the prayer of your loving husband*

*Wesley A Brown*

*Have a lot ready to send when you know where I am. W. Take good care of your health*

On May 14, 1861, the Second Maine boarded trains that took them from Bangor to Portland. Then they traveled by train to Boston, by steamer to New York, and trains to Washington, D.C., where they arrived at three in the morning on June 7. In a month and a half, on July 21, 1861, they would be fully engaged in their first battle.

# FIRST MANASSAS

Wesley's role in the battle and his eyewitness account of First Manassas are recorded in three sources: his 1861 diary, two of his letters to Sabrina, and a letter from the mother of a soldier whose life Wesley saved. From these three sources we can conclude that Wesley was lucky to have survived the battle without being sunstruck or without having suffered a debilitating wound from cannon fire. Despite the awesome physical challenges he endured while caring for himself and another soldier, who surely would have died if Wesley had not helped, he wrote to Sabrina a day or two after the retreat while he was still hungry, filthy, and exhausted. Here is what Wesley wrote in his small, paperback diary about the battle:

*Sunday, July 21, 1861 Pleasant and warm. Got ready to march at 2 AM. Battle commenced at 8 AM lasted until 4 PM when we were obliged to retreat with considerable loss 2$^{nd}$M regt charged on a masked battery 8 times with great bravery so the Generals say. Many men were shot and many wounded. Marched all night so this PM. Marched 60 miles without sleep or anything to eat. At Ft. Cochran tonight. Got wet through today.*

*Tuesday, 23 Pleasant. The rest of the boys that are alive are at Alexandria. Today about 100 are here. We are about used up. Helped a wounded man or I should have been with the regt now. My feet are all blistered over so can hardly step on them.*

*Wednesday, July 24 1861 Pleasant at Arlington Heights.*

Have had nothing but hard bread to eat since the 21$^{st}$. Was ordered to Washington but after going two miles was ordered back.

Thursday, 25 Pleasant. The rest of the regiment joined us today. They all want to go home. Was obliged to burn all my letters before the battle so I feel real lonesome on that account.

Friday, 26 Pleasant. Pitched our tents today on the north side of Fort Cochran. A letter from Brina today. Also one from Aunt Matilda, also GRP of Islesboro.

Here is Wesley's first letter describing his role in the battle of First Manassas, written two days after the battle and while he was nursing blistered feet and hunger at Arlington Heights:

Georgetown DC July 24$^{th}$, 61
My dearest Brina
It is with a thankful heart that I now take my pen in hand to answer your last letter and to assure you that I am well which is more than I can say of many of my brave comrades who but a few days since were with me but are now dead on the Battlefield or are wounded and in the hands of the rebels. We started at 3 PM of the 16$^{th}$ from Falls Church and arrived at Centerville Thursday and stopped until 2 oclock AM of the 21$^{st}$ marched about 2 miles and stopped for 8 hours when our regt. went three miles on the Double quick and charged a masked battery. After firing 4 rounds were obliged to fall back not being supported by the rest of the Brigade but we charged twice more and a part of us went within 40 to 50 ft of the mouth of the cannon when the order was given to retreat. Had we

*been supported we might have taken the battery but that miserable old raunch of our brigade Gen. Tyler meant I believe to have us killed and God only knows what saved so many of us. I fired 15 rounds and I believe I done some _____. The Cannon balls, bullets, shells and grape were whistling round my head like _____ and when I went into the woods a shell fell about 8 ft from me and did not burst which miracle I attribute to your prayers and those of my dear mother. After we retreated I went back in company of some of the boys to carry off the wounded. The man that stood at my right hand was shot dead through the head and the one below him was shot through the heart while the one behind me was wounded and they were falling all around me. But thanks to Providence I am alive and well so is Brother George, Chas Morris, K Taylor, James Coombs, Henry Wheeler, and many more. I guess the missing will amount to about 100.*

*The retreat was a regular Panic, no officer being cool and collected as they should have been. Many were killed by our own men in retreating. I helped off one of our men that was <u>sun struck</u> and we marched about 50 miles that day and night without rest or food but what hurt us much as anything was we run three miles double quick and then fought for so long. We were nearly dead. A part of the regiment are here part in Washington and part in Alexandria. We shall all go to Washington today and I hope to hear from you soon. Had it not been that I was helping a sick man I should have been in Alexandria where most of our boys are.*

*But darling you must not judge of all battles by this one for we did not know where the rebels were and they were hid in the woods and outnumbered us and finally the* *battle was fought three days before <u>Scott</u> intended. We never shall fight that way again. We can whip them if they will come out of the woods and fight where we can see them. A part of the Generals, especially Tyler, can never come off another battle field alive for I believe he is a traitor but Brina no one but you must know that I say so. I cannot write more so good by darling and may providence watch over you. My love to all. Write soon and believe me so ever your affectionate husband and friend Wesley A. Brown.*

*There is a letter inside that you must not read until I get home. Be sure and mind me won't you dearest one. Direct to Washington. <u>Let no one open that letter but me.</u>*

*Write soon and oblige. Wesley*
*I am writing this lying on the ground so excuse all. Tell Luky to write. W.*

We don't have any letters written by Sabrina during the period between the last entry in her diary and October 1861, partly because Wesley burned a number of them. But there is another woman's voice that we hear during the time Sabrina's is absent. It is the voice of a mother, the mother of Union soldier Charles Perkins of Castine, whose life Wesley saved. Mrs. Sewall Perkins wrote a letter to Wesley thanking him for saving her son's life during the chaotic retreat to Washington, D.C., from Bull Run.

The battle of First Manassas, on July 21, was the Second Maine's first experience in battle and they fought well despite their limited training. It was a very hot and humid July day, not the kind of weather that a mid-coast Maine man is used to, and water was not available to the troops during the worst of the fighting. Like others, Charles Perkins became severely dehydrated, sun-struck, delirious, and completely incapable of caring for himself. If Wesley hadn't sought him and taken him in his care, Charles Perkins would surely have died. He shouldered Charles for hours and miles, even as enemy cavalry harassed the remnant of the Union Army during the retreat to Washington, D.C. This was the same battle before which Wesley burned his letters and Henry Wheeler volunteered to retrieve Union wounded under fire. Wesley regretted that even as he assumed responsibility for Charles Perkins' life, he did not have an opportunity to snag a few Confederate souvenirs from the field, as he could see others doing, even during the chaotic retreat. Wesley's souvenir from that day is Mrs. Perkins' letter:

*Castine Aug the 16 1861*
*Mr. Brown.*
*Dear sir permit one, although a stranger to you personally, to return heartfelt thanks for the preservation of my cherished boy, after the late battle, who in all probability would have found an early grave amid the many who sleep their last sleep, but for your kind hand who sought him as a brother's, and led him on the weary march to a place of safety, when darkness surrounded you and you knew not but your own life would pay the forfeit. Words can never repay you, may God's richest blessings rest on you and yours forever and should you ever need a friend may you find such in one as you have proved yourself [to be]. The noblest deed that man could do, casting aside self in an hour of peril, to aid your suffering friend when men were fleeing to save the little life that was left after*

*that horrid day, words cannot express our thanks. God will reward you, may all your future be peace, should it ever be in Our power to repay in kind deeds gladly we will repay. Gold could never be offered a heart so noble, will you kind friend give our sincere thanks to your brother. Charley's letters breathes love toward his officers for their kind treatment in his sickness, he says Lieutenant Brown and Brother have been unto him like Own Brothers will you dear sir continue to care for my lone Boy should he be obliged to remain excuse the mother for writing you. I felt that I must return thanks. My love to all our Soldier Boys. May God guide and protect you and return those who escaped the horrid battle as an unbroken Band to the friends who are waiting and watching with sad hearts. All are well here. My love to Charles. I am writing to him also. The letters did not always reach the friends.*

*Accept a mother's blessing who will pray for you forever. I would like to receive a letter from you if convenient.*
*Your friend,*
*Mrs. Sewall Perkins*

On Monday, July 29, 1861, Sabrina wrote this entry in her journal: *"Rec'd from Wesley in which was account of the late battle in which he took an active part. God bless and save him from the enemy..."*

Judging from the date on Wesley's letter and the date of Sabrina's journal entry, the mail was remarkably efficient. Here is the second letter that Wesley wrote describing his role in the first battle of the Civil War, written while has was recovering from the physical challenges he suffered during the battle and the retreat:

*Arlington Heights Virginia*
*Fort Cochran July 27$^{th}$, 1861*
*Dearest Brina*

*It is with pleasure that I take my pen in hand to scratch a few lines to you in answer to your welcome letters which came in hand yesterday for which accept my sincere thanks, my health is excellent withstanding the forced march of the 21$^{st}$ and 22$^{nd}$, which you may believe was indeed hard. We are now encamped close to Fort Cochran Arlington Heights, but I don't know how long we shall stop here. Most of the boys are clamorous to return home for a "resting spell" but I do not think we shall as yet. If we do we shall be there in August. I wrote you a day or two since and gave you a disconnected account of the battle of the 21$^{st}$, the papers will give you a better idea of it then I can but I made one mistake and that was in regard to CS Morris, he is among the missing but "may turn up yet". I hope and trust he may for I loved him as a friend and he was a good boy. A great many of the boys brought off Secession Guns rifles Swords etc. but I had a sick man in charge and could not bring away anything, although there was plenty of chance to do so as they were scattered all around. I expected to be taken prisoner because with him I could not get along so fast as the rest being obliged to stop to recruit him. He was sun struck and a part of the time delirious—It was with a sad heart that I turned to flee and was against my will but it was unavoidable and here we are. On their part it was well planned, leaving Vienna, Germantown and Fairfax with but little resistance. Their dinners were on the fire almost ready to eat, and we ate it in lieu of them at Fairfax. They kept drawing us on until they got us in the place they wanted* us. It was in a deep valley with masked batteries on every side and then they had 80,000 men to us 20,000. They fought in the woods and would not come out so as to be seen but against all this we should have whipped them if our ammunition had not failed, just as they began to retreat there was not three rounds left for the artillery and without that it was madness to stay as near as we were. Calculate we marched between fifty and sixty miles without food or rest and the only wonder to me is how we stood it but the thoughts of friends sustained many, I know it did for me for if there had been no Brina to have mourned my loss I should have given up. But you must not judge all battles by this as I believe we shall never retreat again for no more hasty and ill-timed battles will be fought, everything will be understood next time—Before the battle I would have wagered my life that we should conquer but it was not to be. For fear of your letters being seen by someone else in case I was shot I burnt every one of them and since that time have felt lonesome on that account, so darling you must write a lot to make up for those, won't you.

There is eight missing out of Co. B. They are Sewall Bowden of Castine, John Dealing of Bangor, Eben Perkins of Brooksville. These we know were shot dead—the missing are CS Morris of Castine, JW King of Bangor, Warren Griffin of Stockton, JD Perkins of Brooksville, Warren Deveraux of Penobscot. The five last may be alive and well—in case anything should happen to me I will say that I have not received a single cent since I left Bangor (ie) from Government. I write this so you may know. The report is that we are to be paid Monday. I must close as I have two more letters to write, one to GRP and one *to Aunt Matilda in West Roxbury—have you received a letter from her yet. She wrote me that she was going to write you—Write real often and long letters won't you Darling one Much love to all friends and believe me as ever your devoted husband Wesley*

Soon after Wesley rested and he was able to reflect on his first experience in battle, he began thinking about his own vulnerability. After all, it is only luck that spares soldiers from injury and death. Wesley had seen enough of battle to know that he could be seriously injured and could have to depend on another to be led off the field or to be nursed for the rest of his life:

*Arlington Heights Va.*
*Camp Rice Aug 3$^{rd}$ 1861*
*Darling wife*
*Don't you think I write to you rather too often! I can't find any fault with you in regard to that. I have received two letters since I got here and have written six to you. My health is quite good at present—Oh! <u>Brina</u> it is so awful lonesome here. The dull monotony of camp life is almost unendurable as there is not much to interest one. If we could have an alarm about once a week it would do... I cannot write any news as there is none. A man was hung on the 2$^{nd}$ for shooting a woman. Please dearest to write often and write real long letters for Wesley won't you. I am much obliged for that paper you sent me. Enclosed with the money is a piece from this morning's National Republican which please to preserve as it is quite a <u>lie</u>. If you have seen the speech that was made when our "California Flag" was presented please*

to preserve it and also the verses if you have not got them send to Minta to get them for you—I expected a letter from you today but was disappointed so I think I'll be ugly and not write again for—oh well, say 24 hours and then I'll ask pardon for my long silence... I cannot keep the foolish thought from my head that if I should return to you maimed or disfigured perhaps lamed for life that you would not love me as well as you now do, that together with my rough associations of mind and matter will I fear unfit one for you as a companion. The first I do not much fear

And I believe that I should prefer death to being either of the three first. My <u>own precious one</u> if I have done wrong in writing the above please to excuse me and when I get home Brina shall pull my ears real hard to pay for it.

P.S. I have looked over the above and see how foolish I am. Should not send it if the mail was not going to start right off don't pay any attention to it and believe me as ever your loving Husband Wesley Write soon. Remember me in love as ever and I thank you for your prayers. Love to all.

Wesley feared that if he returned home seriously disabled and his appearance marred that his marriage would be compromised. In a later letter he wrote, "*I well know that if I should be unfortunate, Brina would willingly <u>labor</u> to support me but there is but little danger of that for if rendered helpless I should deem it my duty to free myself from being a burden to those I love.*" Wesley would have ended his own life to avoid being a burden. Brina's response to these thoughts is not included in the remnant of the correspondence.

# GOSSIP

The marriage went through a crisis during September and October. Sabrina's letters grew infrequent and Wesley grew worried. All he had received from Sabrina were two newspapers—hardly the kind of personal correspondence a lonely soldier needs to be reassured that he's still worth writing to. On September 19, he wrote:

*Three long weeks have elapsed since I have heard one word from you, and words cannot express my anxiety on your account. But I know that you are not sick for today I received two papers form you mailed at New London on the 17th for which I am most thankful but darling* **why don't you write to me** *for I should think that a letter would come as well as a paper but is does not for way down in my heart. I know that you have written as often as once a week and the letters have been miscarried but I trust that I shall soon get an answer to the 7th that I have sent to you to Groton as that is the number and one that I mailed to Islesboro with a letter from Mother... if this reaches you before you start for home I shall be thankful for I don't think you have got all my letters or you would have written...*

It is an age-old complaint between correspondents that one side in the exchange does not write as often as the other would like. Generally, people like to receive personal correspondence. A homesick soldier depends on correspondence as his link to hearth and home. If the letters stop, anxiety could be replaced by fear: fear of abandonment, fear of love lost, fear of powerlessness. It's easy to imagine the anxiety a soldier must feel when, besides having to worry about his own mortality, he must also worry about the loyalty of his spouse. Sabrina's silence or unwillingness to write might have been due to some anxiety on her own part. Five months after Wesley left Islesboro, Sabrina became deeply troubled by a piece of island gossip. Wesley must have sensed her distress because of the tone of a letter she wrote dated September 26, soon after she returned from Connecticut. We don't have that letter but judging from Wesley's response it seems that something Sabrina heard was bothering her, but she didn't reveal any more than that and she didn't include specifics until Wesley pressed her on it. In reply to Sabrina's letter of September 26, Wesley questioned her concerning the source of her distress and tried to reassure her that whatever lie was being spread around, it couldn't be any worse than the usual brand of island gossip.

> *Fort Cochran Va*
> *Oct 5 1861*
> *My Ever Dear Brina*
> *It is with pleasure that I now sit down to answer your most kind and welcome letter of Sept. 26th which came to hand last evening and I assure you never was letter read with more pleasure than was that. At the same time I read one from Luky also one from Charles.*
> *I think from the tone of yours that you must of heard something to ruffle your usually quiet and even-balanced mind, for I know that a trifle would not thus disturb you for few women have so good mind with so sound judgment as my own dear wife. But darling you must not be paying attention to such idle gossip as I know abounds in*

*Islesboro, at all times, and more especially when a person is absent for a short time. I believe you know all this without my writing it, do you not dearest. No, Brina must not care for them but laugh their slander to scorn—*

*I know dearest that it is hard to bear all their gossip in silence when you know that some of it is done by enemies on purpose to annoy you and you cannot conjecture of the pain that it gives me when I think that you are there alone to bear it all and that too at a time when any gentleman of lady should try to make your lot as easy as possible, and either would, I know very well that they cannot say anything to hurt you, because all your friends and enemies know that you are above doing anything that merits slander and reproach, if I except the act of marrying such a good for nothing fellow as myself. Me they can gossip about and no one knows me, or at least many do not, and they can lie as much as they please about me when I am absent and no one can refute their foul slander. And I know it must pain you to hear them but tis my wish for you not to mind it more than possible as the ones that talk like that are no more worthy of notice of Brina than Jeff Davis is to sit in Lincoln's seat and them same persons are worse traitors than Jeff is for they, under the guise of friendship, assail in the tenderest part of a person's character while Davis comes out in open warfare, but I fear I shall weary you if I continue on this subject so I will change it...*

Wesley was not aware of the gravity of the gossip. He even thought that it might have been about Sabrina, but the gossip was about him, mainly, though Sabrina was deeply hurt by it. The gossip was this: that Wesley left

Sabrina to join the Union Army because he was dissatisfied with his wife and married life. Since Wesley was off the mark in his assumptions about the content of the gossip, Sabrina had to confront her husband. After some talk about the weather and a summary of conversations during recent visits with close relatives, we read this:

*Well, my dear, there was something to disturb me a little when I last wrote you, something beside the mere sound of your deserting and being taken etc—something dearest more heartaching to one than those absurd stories...[pertaining] to your leaving but I knew you better and wasn't I glad I did...*

*But my dear will you allow me to ask you a question or two...in regard to that. You say that when you return you will be happy etc. Wesley it was by your request that I write—what I am going to say and perhaps it will be no harm and make me feel better too thought I should never have told you those absurd stories if Luky hadn't before I was aware of it for I thought they would worry you and result in no good. But to proceed:*

*Were you always happy after our marriage? And did you never sigh for single blessedness, and wish that thyself and Brina had remained twain forever/ But dearest to come to the point did you ever say to any person walking this earth that you did not enjoy the married life and unhappiness with me was the chief cause of your enlistment. I say, did ever aught like that escape your lips to any living mortal—I shall not tell you now where I learned of it but was from a source the veracity of which the public would fail to question. Wesley, I implore you in the name of all that's good to tell me if ever such escaped your lips. Wes-*

*ley, if ever there was anything that made me unhappy, yea wretched, it was that. O dearest I can never tell you what those words caused me and if I seen you I should have been willing to die. O yes For then memory would have caused to recall those burning words. For two nights I tossed an unhappy heartaching victim upon my pillow vainly wanting sleep until last midnight when I arose in the stillness and lighted the lamp and tried to write. Yes I wrote my feelings as near I could on paper and have it now...*

It seems unusually cruel to tell a wife that her husband enlisted because he was dissatisfied with his marriage. This implies that Wesley used the war as an excuse to leave Brina because he was dissatisfied with Sabrina herself. No wife needs to be told this at any time, but especially when her husband is not present to counter the claim, and it makes the claim an attack on the husband as well. Wesley was in a fix. He was fighting two wars: one against the Confederates and one against the scourge of island gossip. It was easier for him to defend himself from rebel guns than it was for him to engage his enemies on Islesboro. He had to respond with the greatest care and honesty through his careful choice of words. He was forced to commit his full attention to Sabrina's letter because this was a crisis that could be resolved only through the mail.

*Cull's Hill*
*Camp Jameson Oct 17$^{th}$/61*
*Dear Wife*
*With pleasure I now take my pen to acknowledge the rect. Of your welcome letter of the 13$^{th}$ which came to hand*

last evening, also one from "Brother Bob". I was glad to get one from him as it made all matters plain and satisfactory and I wrote to him

Before breakfast this morning, and I must be short with this as the regt has formed a line of battle and we are on guard so we do not go out now unless attacked. But I will come to the point. You say that Nelson is going to pay you some money and advises you to invest it in a vessel where it will pay he thinks from 20-50 per cent while a savings bank pays only _____. My darling Brina, you seem to anticipate what my answer will be viz your money was left you by your father to use as you saw fit. I know that your judgment is good in regard to such matters. Were it otherwise I might, if asked, give my advice but as matters are situated now I cannot advise in the least, as it would be wrong for me to do so. All I wish is for it to do you as much good as possible, and our children, if blest with any. I may never return home, and if not I do not wish to have it said that I advised you to place your money only as your own mind dictated. You, however, had better use the whole of it for if my life is spared I shall send home all I earn which will pay your board if nothing more. Your money I know nothing about neither the _____ and I am sorry you asked me about investing it, for if I do not tell you it will make you feel bad and I cannot in honor now do it. If you should by any mismanagement lose every cent of it no word or thought of mine would ever chide you for it. So darling you must act your own mind in regard to it just as you would have done a year ago. It may seem odd that I do not say anything about it but to tell the truth I should have done it had it not been for the last part of your letter. Now for that:

*I never said aught like that to any being, never thought like that anything of the kind and had I done so, never should have said it to anyone. If I ever return I want to see what you wrote those two nights when you _____. You demand to know for certain about it. May God direct the first ball that is fired straight to my heart and may my soul forever remain in punishment if I have ever said anything of the kind and it surprises me to think that you would credit such stuff. If my own mother whom I deem truth itself should say such things of you I could not believe it but because some person or persons who you know to be gossipers tell you a few lies about me you make yourself wretched for weeks. You must deem me deceitful for every letter has expressed my heart's feelings and them were pure love and respect for you. Since our marriage my love has if possible increased for you nothing but joy and thankfulness ever passed my mind (much less my lips) that I had been so fortunate as to obtain your loved hand and heart. Tis I know more than I deserve for I know I am not all that Brina merits. For I have not riches nor learning but I have an honest heart and you possess the whole of it. I know that I never done anything that should lead you to believe such stories as you wrote me. But I am very glad that you let me know of it for it may relieve your mind. But hereafter you must remember that I have but one friend to who I disclose such heart feelings as that purports to be and that friend is my own loved wife. Now I want to know the author of such slander, as that is your duty to let me know, and I trust that you will do so let me know all the particulars, every word, so I may know all of the details of such stuff. The happiest month of my life was from the 28th of March to the 24th of April,*

1861. Never can I express in words the joy I felt at that time. Mortal could not be happier and my dearest, my wish is that you may ever be as happy as we then were. It was not because I did not enjoy the married life that I enlisted; it was because I loved my country and was willing to sacrifice the newfound joy of life and everything for her, my country's honor. It was the hardest thing I ever done, to part with you darling. It seemed worse than separating my _____ but loved wife. I may never more press my lips to that loved cheek, may never fold you again in my arms and go to sleep happy as a man could be. But whatever befalls me be assured that my love is not Passion, know that my respect, love and well wishes was with you to the last. I do not chide you for writing me all about that. I am very thankful that you did. I do not blame you for believing it either. You could not do otherwise if it came from a reliable source, after what has been told and you did not know me but you should know that I abhor deceit and had I thought anything like that my letters would have showed it—darling. I am lying on my bunk writing so you must excuse this. I must close this as it is time to go on duty. You must let me know who reported that story won't you dearest and when the war is ended I'll return to love and happiness and I know that Brina will welcome me won't she. Write soon dear one and be careful of your health so as to be on hand to greet your sojer boy when he returns. Write very often and write long letters. Hoping this will reach you with safety. I remain yours as ever, W.

Even before she received that letter, Sabrina wrote to Wesley on October 19 from Castine, saying:

*Wesley don't mind what I wrote in my last letter about that story I heard. I regret writing anything about it but by your request but it made one feel very bad at heart for awhile. Now I don't allow myself to think anything about it. I didn't let anyone know at the time that I deemed any of those absurd stories worthy of notice. But when alone and in the still watches of the night they would haunt one like so many unearthly spirits. But they have had their time as does everybody and everything. Revel for a season then pass away. But I do not mourn for their return.*

So when Sabrina received Wesley's letter, she had already asked him to minimize the seriousness of the gossip and assured him that she was able to get beyond the pain of the moment. When Wesley's letter came, it must have provided Sabrina the comfort she needed to get beyond the memory of having confronted her husband concerning the truth about his feelings for her.

There's no reason to think that Wesley enlisted for anything other than patriotic reasons. All we need to do is read Henry's letter to his cousin to sense the depth of loyalty Maine men attached to the Union—a loyalty that demanded, if necessary, the sacrifice of one's life. We also recall how moved Wesley was by Edward Everett's speech about George Washington. His patriotism was sincere. There being no children might have made the decision to enlist easier. Wesley's decision was not made without balancing the joys of married life with the risks inherent in defending his country's honor. After all, he did say that deciding to join was "the hardest thing I ever done."

Sabrina's next paragraph contains entirely different

subject matter, suggesting that the crisis is over and new thoughts are coming to mind. She shares her fascination with an 1820 painting titled *The Court of Death* by Rembrandt Peale. When researching ancient literature, such an abrupt change of subject might be a clue that a different writer altogether has inserted his own work anonymously into a letter or poem so that his contribution would circulate with its host's text. Sabrina's discussion of *The Court of Death* is similarly abrupt but this is probably because Sabrina wrote the paragraph later in the day, maybe after having seen a copy of the painting somewhere in Castine earlier. *The Court of Death* paragraph reveals a dark and brooding dimension to Sabrina's character and, it being wartime, it seems almost inappropriate to share such sentiments with a soldier who was trying to come to terms with the idea that he might not return home.

# THE COURT OF DEATH

Sabrina wrote:
...*What an all absorbing and interesting picture of deep and thoughtful study is The Court of Death. I think it the most sublime and awe striking picture it was ever my lot to behold. Death personified looks so much like death, dark sublime solemn and grim. I could study it for hours and never weary. One of these days I will buy one; when I have a copy home to place in my sanctum and find there something to gaze upon which will be in harmony with my care worn feelings. You say when you hope to return Brina won't have care enough to make her wish for anything so dark and somber looking as that. Yes dearest I should, for my nature is such that let me be surrounded by friends dear as thee and with all the pleasure of life also and there would be times when solitude with something upon which to satiate the mind like the Court of Death would have more charms for me than all else though I aught and will except you, I say friends as dear as thou art. I mistake for I have none so dear [within], can I. For I know to be near you to hear your voice to gaze on your precious self to drink of the love that has often flowed in thy liquid eye would be an endless source of happiness, a fountain of secret joy to me though at the same time I might to all appearances be forgetful of your presence. I can cite times now before our marriage when you seemed cold to me cold and indifferent, while I enjoyed such a secret happiness, happy because I was near you.*

*I have been washing dishes for Emma and what do you suppose we had for dinner. Something you like first-rate and we wished you had some. It was scallop chowda and was very nice. I never ate any before in chowda.*

*I dreamed of you last night. I thought you come home and I had a nice time.*

*It has been storming all day.*

*That was a false story I heard in regard to E—She is not a Bostonian for which I am very glad.*

*I presume I had a letter come to the island last night from you. I have not rec'd any for a week but E rec'd [one] so I heard from you via others. I don't know what else to write now so I guess I'll close. Please tell me in your next letter if you think Gen Fremont merits all the censure that the press has been showering on him for the last two months. I don't think he does. Write soon Direct to N Islesboro. Write often <u>every day</u>, good by from your loving wife, Brina*

Sabrina mentions a sanctum in which she would someday place or hang a copy of *The Court of Death*. A sanctum could be a room, a shelf, a space on a mantle, or a container of any size and shape. It is private space for storage or display of objects of intense personal meaning. These objects might encourage reflection on universal themes or simply recall moments in the past for quiet amusement or to repel loneliness. Sabrina had to learn about this custom from someone and she probably learned it from one of her two mothers, or both. Wesley's backpack was a sanctum for his letters from Sabrina and after Wesley died, Sabrina's trunk was a sanctum for Wesley's letters: "Don't take them out of the chest, will you, Luky. They are letters from Wesley and as such are sacred to me."

# SOMETHING LIKE SEX

Sabrina's comment about having dreamed about Wesley created a passionate response. His letter dated November 9 includes a reference to a nocturnal visitor:

*Shall I tell you what I dreamed the night before last? Well, I took off my pants for the first night since I left Maine, and after going to sleep I dreamed I was in bed with Brina at home and thought I was <u>kissing</u> her so you guess the consequences my draws were not in presentable shape the next morning, <u>hardly</u>, but if I had been with you I should have taken them off before I <u>retired</u>, <u>shouldn't</u> I.*

Sabrina's expressions of affection are more reserved but she could be kittenish: "I must soon say goodnight pleasant dreams to you, with a good warm sleep. I wish you was here so I could snuggle you and keep you warm and myself too for I thought I would freeze last night and O didn't I wish for you, for you would be as good as a dozen mill blankets which is the warmest kind of bed clothing." It was an amusing comment—that her husband was as good as a dozen mill blankets—as if the value of any person could be measured so.

Once, Wesley used his rifle to create a sexual innuendo:

*Darling One, I beg you will be more careful in the future about getting cold, especially at that time of each month so that you may not suffer so much, for it makes me feel real bad to know that <u>my Brina</u> is suffering when perhaps if I was there to guard her that it would* *not be so, as I am a good sentry, with my <u>rifle</u> and other <u>munitions of war.</u> I might fire my rifle if I get <u>excited</u>, don't you believe it dearest. O yes I would be very watchful and no harm should come near thee when I was by—*

One wonders how creative Wesley could have been using a cannon as his inspiration!

Wesley even managed to compare a game of checkers with moves associated with love-play:

*...this evening I have been playing checkers and did not get beaten very bad. I wish I could be home to play with you (checkers I mean). I should move my man (men I mean) into the King row very quickly and then you would have to crown him (them I mean). I believe I used to beat you at <u>checkers</u>. I generally got my men crowned first—*

In his letter from Hall's Hill, Virginia, dated February 13, 1862, Wesley reveals his interest in having a child but he wraps the subject in the guise of a joke. These are sad lines for readers not just because we know that Wesley will never be a father, but because the subject is being used by him to create a reputation for virility that would impress his comrades:

*...Will Griffin says he will name your baby Fanny as he is acquainted with a nice girl by that name and I promised him he should name the first child that I was father to. Henry Wheeler came in here last evening and made my messmates believe that you was mother to a fine girl child. Ha! Ha! Ha! You will have to scold him for doing so when you see him as they all firmly believe it is so. Well*

*dearest one if my ears was within reach of your hands I should expect to see any amount of stars, but you will have to reserve your punishment until I return, when I intend to make you forget all about them, won't I.*

Wesley did not deny he had become a father of a girl and he let his comrades believe it was so. He knew that Sabrina might be miffed by the lie—enough to wring his ears if she were at his side—but he let the fiction stand because he liked the feeling that his comrades thought that he was a father.

We assume that Wesley and Sabrina consummated their marriage during the month that they were living as a married couple, but no pregnancy resulted from that union. To lead others to believe that a successful pregnancy did result during so short a period of time would suggest that Wesley was a potent lover and boost his reputation for manliness. Among fellow warriors who shared stories of wives and lovers, that reputation might have strengthened Wesley's self-confidence. Still, it's sad to think that Wesley nurtured the lie and, ironically, died without progeny.

## "... THE VICISSITUDES OF A SOLDIER'S LIFE..."

After the gossip crisis was resolved in late October 1861, Sabrina was inclined to write longer letters. Only one of her letters, dated February 13, 1862, survived the months between December 22 and August 14, 1862. Unfortunately, she encouraged Wesley to burn some of her letters and we know Wesley was, understandably, willing to oblige so he could reserve space in his backpack. Because of this dearth of letters from Sabrina's pen, it is important to read her letter of October 23, 1861—a letter that she asked Wesley to burn, but he spared it. In this letter we are introduced to the faith of a young woman in mid-nineteenth century coastal Maine:

*My Dearest Wesley*

*It is evening and has been storming through the day but cleared off beautifully. I presume if Emma [George Brown's wife] and I had our way about the weather today it would have been pleasant but no, the Clerk would give us no such authority over the scared laws of nature. What a blessing it is to the human race that they cannot always have their way. What a world this would be if everyone could have the slightest wish their own way and realize every sigh. How many times since you left Islesboro would you have been transported thither from Washington if ever Brina's wishes had been gratified. The South would long ago since been subjugated if the unanimous wish of the North had been gratified. The North would have been a great mass of decaying bodies and mouldering ruins with Jeff Davis and accomplices holding an* inquest. O what a world this might be, more blest than days of yore! How many very absurd and foolish wishes we make in the course of a month, yea a day, many which if gratified would ultimately change the whole tenor of our lives, perhaps for the better, perhaps for the worse.

We often make a wish which at the time would seem to make us happy but in some future it might be the instrument of making us perfectly miserable. How thankful then we aught to be that there is an All-wise, All seeing, and All knowing disposing God, who has ordered from the beginning everything for the best, even to my husband's going to the war. But if such an insignificant or narrow minded shortsighted humanity as myself had had her wishes gratified there would have been at the close of our national contest one the less "laurel wreath" to lay down their arms, having done all required help to retrieve their nation's honor. So is the world made up of wishes, disappointments, sighs, tears, hopes, joys, sorrows and numerous other from the class of "light and shade" included, which God in his wise providence bestows upon each and all, now giving one cup of joy overflowing with health, love, friends, honor, riches etc then bestowing upon another less fortunate in life, a cup of afflicting sorrow, filled and steeped with the dregs of disappointment, blasted hopes, pinching poverty, cooling friendships, dying friends, sorrowing remorse, heartaching regrets etc. God is just, then why this difference? Is it that his name may be honored and glorified on earth? It is. He is All Wise, giving to each and all their just deserts, having, perhaps, far in the distance beyond the conception of the human mind some great good which is being wrought out by his mysterious workings among the posterity of Adam.

*Man proposes, he thinks, hopes, anticipates, builds castles, plants one here another there. His great ships cut the waters of every ocean while his coffers are daily filling with the hoarded "yellow dust" thereby making him great and powerful among the secular world. He will study and search after "hidden treasures" striving to immortalize and enroll his name upon the pages of fame. All this man proposes and much, very much more does he accomplish. But how often does the great God see fit to dispose of it all and the "proposer" man too. There, Brina, you are always getting off some such great long preamble out of nothing. Well my precious husband I wanted to write something to fill up this paper and so I wrote a few thoughts as they occurred but that will do for this time. Now for a peep at Emma and Brina here in the kitchen. You know there is a table sits in the corner of the room. Well I sit at the end of it with the hat on my head for a light screen and a penholder in hand which consists of a stick with a pen tied to it with a piece of red thread...Emma sits at the side of the table reading her letter that she is writing to George. Her light screen is that soljer hat George sent home which he obtained at "bull run". She has one foot on the cradle rocking her "bunch of sugar plums..."*

*I have been sewing the heels of a pair of socks to send you today with some others. Well, darling Wesley, Brina must say pleasant dreams to you and one of my wishes is to tuck you in your cozy bunk. Now is it cozy or not and if so is there room enough for someone the size of Brina... Brina must stop now for it is long past now—from your you know who!*

*And grant me the favor of destroying this scroll with several others—if not already gone. Please do so. Brina.*

Here was a picture of two young women in Castine, Maine, writing to their husbands who were serving in the Union Army. One was a mother, the other not a mother yet and who wouldn't be a mother by the man to whom she was married at that time.

Sabrina told Wesley that his letters rarely contained expressions of discouragement, frustration, and regret. Though Wesley regularly complained about loneliness and confessed that he missed his wife, Sabrina seems to have expected her husband to express a broader scope of feelings in his letters. Even in modern relationships, this observation is not infrequently brought to light by one party or the other.

*Nov. 10, 1861*
*My Dearest Husband*
*As I am left this cloudy PM minus company I will devote a short space of time to the answer of your blessed epistle of the 2nd which was duly recd last night and perused with great pleasure though it was written during that horrid storm its tome manifests nothing but the calm quiet which seems ever to pervade the noble breast of my far off soldier. My dear, why is it that your letters all seem so free from care and mental depression when certainly if I understand your impulsive nature there must be times when thy heart will be heavy and thy brow shaded by care. If care doth ever visit you it is not frequent when you write to me, or, if it is, you keep it safely locked in your own breast as sacred from the keys of her who now writes. In all thy letters there is no murmuring against officers or those of the company, no regrets that you ever enlisted, no serious apprehensions of a soldier's death, no wishes*

*to be with the loved at home, and no murmurings against the war's tardy progress but all as calm as the ticking of yonder clock. My dear you be careful and...*

Sabrina was mystified that Wesley expressed no fear for his life, no confession of longing for his wife, no anger about the way the war was being prosecuted, and no complaints about the men with whom he lived and from whom he took orders. He complained about the boredom of picket duty but never cursed his lot as a private in the Union Army. He reserved his anger for Captain Sprague of Islesboro, the mail carrier whom Wesley accused of tampering with his letters to Sabrina. Wesley's temper only rose when he perceived that his sole link to his wife was threatened by unethical mail carriers.

So the country entered its first winter as a nation at war with itself. The Second Maine wintered in Hall's Hill, Virginia, no farther then ten miles from Washington, D.C. They would decamp in March and participate in the siege of Yorktown in April. For now, the soldiers decorated their camp with evergreens, in a kind of elaborate gothic fashion, and had their photograph as a regiment taken sometime around Christmas. Wesley described the scene in his letter dated December 25:

*Dearly beloved wife: Christmas Eve of 1861 finds me a great deal farther away from you than I ever expected it would when one year ago about this hour we were happy in each other's society and were laying plans for our future life, but our plans are for the present forestalled but I hope only for a season as I hope ere the New Year ends to be again with you never again to be parted except by* death. My health is good as need be and George has entirely recovered his health—

For the past two days we (ie CoB) have been ornamenting our company ground and we have it looking as nice as can be. If I was good describing I would tell you how it is fixed. Perhaps you may get some idea of it if I try to tell you—

Over the entrance to our street is a large arch thirty feet high and (including the smaller arches) twenty feet wide. On each side of this and connected to it is smaller arches, the whole wreathed with cedar in the center of the large arch is a large star wreathed in Evergreen. In one of the smaller arches is a circular wreath with the figure 2 inside of it. In the other is a similar one with the letter B. All of Evergreen and a kind of green tree that we found in a garden here. Then on each side in the rear of the tents is a thick layer of small cedar trees and over the two tents of the officers is arches and between their tents and ours is a hedge with two arches in it. There darling can you understand that poor description. I don't think I could—

I don't think I never saw anything so neat and pretty. A few rods distant one can hardly see a tent but after the arch is passed our homes can be seen looking as cozy as can be. Besides looking well it keeps off the winds so now we do not fear a snow storm if one should chance to come. Gen Martindale complimented us very highly on its beauty today.

Well darling one how have you passed the day. Was it pleasant or stormy. Did you take a sleigh ride or stay home. What did you have for dinner today. I had nothing, only what we get every day—

*I expected to receive a Christmas present from you today but got disappointed. I expected to get that diary by tonight's mail but did not. I wrote to you last Friday also last Saturday. I read an extra letter from you last Saturday night and then you were very much worried about my cold. Do not let that fret you any more for it has gone—Oh Brina. Guess what I done this morning when it was cold enough to freeze water. Well I stripped naked and washed myself all over. It was a cold job I assure you but after it was over I felt well enough to repay me. I went down to the woods and done it. Dearest don't you think we have had a remarkably warm winter so far. Water has never got frozen hard enough to bear me up out here. I should have sent you a gift if I could have got anything to send but you know how it is. We are tied right here and cannot get away—I must close now for it is getting chilly—*

*Take good care of your health and write me a good long letter New Year's Day and darling I again wish you a very happy New Year with many kind wishes I remain yours truly, Wesley*

*Hall's Hill*
*Camp Jameson Jan 1$^{st}$ 1861*

*Dearest Brina*
*I will greet you by wishing you a Happy New Year and may it indeed prove a happy one to you my darling wife. I hope that no clouds of sorrow may dim your Horizon but that during the present year all will be sunshine and happiness with you.*

*I have been for the past week expecting that diary but it*

*has not come yet nor have I rec'd a letter from you for two weeks, only an old one that was written the 8$^{th}$ Dec though that was welcomed with joy for it came from your hand. I do not think that your letters reach _____ for that was written the 8$^{th}$ of the month and was not mailed until the 25$^{th}$.*

*I enjoy good health with the exception of a slight cough which is growing better. George is well as is Henry W. and they both send regards.*

*If you wish to know what your "Sojer boy" had for New Years dinner we had a bread pudding with plenty of raisins and butter also sugar in it (ie our mess) Then we had a good vegetable soup and plenty of bread and cheese so I guess I had almost as good as Brina did, didn't I darling?*

*...Well dearest the mail has arrived and yet no letters. I wish I knew if you were sick although I hope tis only faults of the mail that I do not hear from you. Yet I fear that you are sick—I have done up my diary to send to you and shall send it as I hear from you. I want you to buy a new one of 1861 and copy from this one and write it down in ink so I can look at it years hence and tell just where I have been every day...*

*As ever yours, Wesley*

Wesley's diaries recorded his location each day and probably not much else. Though the discovery of such a diary would fascinate a Civil War historian, it might not contain the personal material we read in his letters. A partial diary dated 1861 is in the collection but his 1862 diary was lost on the march to Groveton, Virginia, where Second Manassas was fought.

Christmas and the New Year found Wesley bereft

of new letters from Sabrina. Absence from home during the holiday season can be discouraging—especially in the service—and the tone of Wesley's letters was not improved by waiting weeks for a letter from Sabrina. On January 5, Wesley wrote, *"Yesterday a man belonging to the 18th Mass regt shot himself being as he said homesick. He was a married man and had been for the past few days wandering in his mind. He had just come off guard and said to his comrades, 'Well boys I shant be with you long. Whoever gets my wife will get a good one,' and went away a few rods and shot himself in the heart."*

Most people who use a gun to kill themselves seem to target the head but the soldier from Massachusetts shot himself in the part of his body that hurt the most: his lovelorn heart.

For months, Wesley pursued an opportunity to have his picture taken so he could send it to Sabrina. References to pictures, ambrotypes, and daguerreotypes were frequent in the correspondence and Wesley was very particular about the way he wanted to look when he finally had a picture taken that he deemed satisfactory to send to Sabrina. He was fully prepared when the opportunity arrived in mid-January. He had an ambrotype taken while he was dressed in full gear. He included a description of each strap and item visible in his picture:

*January 17th 1862*
*Dear Brina*
*I now sit down to pen you a few lines to explain the use of the straps that you see crossing my body in the accompanying ambrotype. The one that goes over my left*

*shoulder across my breasts carries my cartridge box. The smallest one over my right shoulder is my canteen and the other one is my knapsack in which we carry rations. The two that go over my shoulders and are attached together in front by a cross belt are my knapsack straps. The top of the knapsack can just be seen over my shoulders. The belt that goes round my waist keeps my cartridge belt steady and carries my Cap box and bayonet sheath. The upper brass plate is an eagle, the lower one has V.M.M. on it. My hat is turned up on one side and a feather on the other. The face you will recognize I guess. I thought I would send a good case, although the price rather costly in Virginia—The whole please to accept from Wesley P.S. I wrote you last night and sent a map of the Southern States. So now good by as ever yours—W.*

No image of Wesley exists in the correspondence or in the archives. Maybe Sabrina distributed daguerreotypes or tintypes of Wesley to his family after she remarried. If this were the case, the two places where pictures of Wesley might be are in Bangor, Maine, or Monticello, Wisconsin.

Battles were not fought during winter so a soldier had more time to write. When Wesley had the time, he would write longer, more reflective letters. In the following letter, he worries that military life will change his character for the worse. Thoughts of his own mortality return and he suggests that Sabrina remarry after a year or so if he dies in battle, if she finds a man who loves her at least as much as he did:

*Camp Jameson*
*Hall's Hill Va Feb 8th 1862*

*Dearly Loved Wife*

...You say in yours that you shall be very happy to place yourself under my care, but darling I fear that I shall not be as tender and careful as I should be in guarding so precious a treasure. I was but poorly fitted for that noble work ere I enlisted in my Country's service, and after having been out here two or three years I shall not be so tender and watchful as I should be in caring for you, whom I love far better than life. I fear that camp life will make me <u>rough</u>, and unfit me for the society of ladies and especially for domestic life. Tis so [monotonous] and so irritating to one of my temperament, it will make me fractious I fear—

But if I keep on in this way it will make you <u>dread</u> my return rather than look forward to it with pleasure, for you know I was disagreeable <u>enough</u> ere I left home. Well darling, when I return I will try and be good <u>always</u> and I want you if I ever have by <u>word</u> or <u>deed</u> wounded your feelings to forget it and never think about it again. I know that I sometimes when at home was <u>disagreeable</u> and I sometimes write fractious letters all such please to burn, and forget they were ever sent.

I wrote to you last Wednesday eve and I was about sick having been on hard duty for three or four days. I do not expect it was a very good letter. You ask me if I ever think of you when I retire at night with my bedfellow. Oh! Yes darling. I assure you I always do and never have I went to sleep without asking our "Heavenly Father" to watch over your slumbers and keep you safe from harm. I am not fit to pray for myself but I believe that to pray for one so pure and good as yourself makes me better. You ask if I expect to meet you in heaven if it should be my lot to fall on the battle field. No, darling, <u>heaven</u> according to

<u>your idea</u> and my <u>belief</u> was not intended for such as me. I shall never reach that degree of perfection that <u>I think</u> is requisite to carry one to that place that you merit and will obtain when you die. Not by my own efforts surely, but it may be, that the prayers of an angel wife and a sainted mother may carry me there. I <u>hope</u> so at least for I should want no <u>other happiness</u> than to be <u>with you</u> through all time...

    I wish you had had your ink so as to of written me that midnight epistle for I should of liked it real well and then how nice it would seem to have Brina in her bedroom all alone writing to me. Why if she wrote me a real <u>loving</u> and <u>confidential</u> letter it would seem almost like being with her, only you would have no one to give your sweet, thrilling kisses to and no one to repay them with interest as Wesley would and will as soon as it is our good fortune to again be pressed in each others arms, to feel your warm loving heart pressed against mine, to feel your sweet lips and loving kisses on mine and hear you say you are all mine. Oh yes darling one that will indeed be a pleasure to which I look forward as does the shipwrecked sailor to the sighting of land——————I heartily wish that I could be invisible and hear some of your soliloquies when alone in the fields or woods. I wish you would pen me a real nice loving letter you know what I mean, just such a one as you would of done that night that you forgot your ink—Darling if it should be my lot to fall on the battlefield you must bear up with a brave heart and you will in a year or so find someone that you will love and who will act the part of protector much better than I have done but be assured that my last thought and prayer will be for your welfare and happiness—

*Yes darling I read the little book that you gave me very often, and I intend to as long as it holds together and then I shall get another...*
*So now goodnight darling and believe me as ever Truly Yours, Wesley*
   *write soon and often, W.*

The joy that Wesley felt from sending his portraits was compromised by his brooding and reflective mood. It was midwinter, after all, and Wesley was feeling glum and distracted. Sabrina sensed this and encouraged him to recover:

*N Islesboro Feb 13$^{th}$ '62*
*My Dear Wesley*
*Yours of the 5$^{th}$ came to hand last night and though it left you in very poor spirits and a very bad headache—yet it found Brina in pretty good spirits, entertaining company, but after reading yours it put kind of a damper on my spirits for I felt at a loss to know why my Wesley would cherish such an idea in situation to my receiving those miniatures of yourself. Truly if I never received anything _____ the pleasure it was those facsimiles of your dear, and to me, priceless self... And my dear you mistake when you say I called the 1$^{st}$ miniature a poor thing. I said something to this effect: that you had changed somewhat and for that reason did not look as well as one taken when you was Wesley and that ambrotype I think is grand good looking picture and if I mistake not I have experienced more than the same before. The photographs are very perfect indeed. I think them very pretty, forsooth real handsome don't you think so. I know you do by the way*

*you wrote. Well, darling, receive a slight rebuke from one and then we'll let the miniature ripples flow away into the tide of forgotten memories...*

Wesley's spirit must have recovered because in his letter of February 12, he doesn't mention the slight he believed he received from Sabrina. In this same letter, he asked Sabrina if she would look into his tool chest to see if his tools were rusting—the tools that he told Sabrina she must not loan to anybody because he would return in the fall or spring. He knew from what Sabrina said in her letter that the passage of time and the stress of duty had changed his appearance and now he was worried about the condition of things that he would use to support himself and Sabrina if he ever returned home. He now knew that the war could last longer than he thought it would when he enlisted. Still, he felt optimistic that he would be one of the lucky soldiers who might just make it home without serious injury. On March 10 he wrote, "*...so darling don't be worried on my account will you. For after passing through what I did on the 21$^{st}$ of July last I believe that the bullet is not yet moulded that will harm me.*" Wesley was absolutely right: that bullet had not yet been moulded, but it would be.

Spring arrived, winter camp was struck, and the war resumed.

By June, Wesley learned that Sabrina was going to move off of the island, but because so little of her correspondence from this time remains, we don't know her reasons for wanting to leave. She would have had to wait for the end of the school year because she was teaching. She had in mind that she wasn't going to return for awhile and if she did, it would have been as a guest of her sister,

Luky, who remained on the island. She might have found the lifestyle and company of her relatives in Castine and Bangor more comfortable. Wesley's Uncle Cyrus in Bangor was a prosperous man and Sabrina spent weeks at a time living with his family. Emma Brown of Castine, George Brown's wife, was a good friend and she and Sabrina were good company for each other. Wesley frequently told Sabrina to live where she was most comfortable—that her place of residence was her choice—and it seems she was more comfortable on the mainland than on the island. Wesley knew the move involved risk and worried about the safety of her passage across the bay:

*Gaines Mill, Va, June 5$^{th}$ 1862*
*...I fear you may attempt to cross over to Castine in a small boat and at this time of year it is not safe especially for one so loaded as you and your effects would load one. If still on the Island do not attempt the passage unless in a large boat attended by a skillful boatman. Above all do not take that chest of tools into the same boat that you go in, as it will be a dead weight in case of a tempest it could greatly endanger your life. You had better hire Mr. \_\_\_\_ to carry that over some other time or someone else...*

Sabrina moved to Castine without incident and settled into Emma's house, a place where a young family lived, where Sabrina could be useful and where she could enjoy the companionship of a woman whose husband was also away at war. Wesley's tool chest remained on the island for another five months.

While Sabrina was living with Emma in Castine, Wesley was fighting in Virginia during McClellan's Peninsula Campaign. This campaign was designed to capture Richmond, the Confederate capital. One of the battles in which Wesley fought during that time was near Hanover Court House on May 27, 1862. This was as violent a battle as any during the war, with advantage traded back and forth between sides and the Second Maine was in the heaviest of it. The Union prevailed. Five days after the battle, Wesley wrote:

> *Gaine's Mill, Va. June 2$^{nd}$/62*
> *...I feared that you would be very anxious after the battle if I did not write, but now I am well and healthy as a buck and can eat my full rations. In the Battle of May 27$^{th}$ our regt. had three hundred men engaged and we had thirty-nine killed and wounded. Co. B had seven wounded and one killed, Sergt SC _____ of Castine, a good and worthy man, but he leaves a large family who depended on him for their living. I was with him just before he died. He said that if his family was provided for he should die willingly but to leave them without a protector it seemed hard to him. Four others of our company was badly wounded, one had a leg amputated, another was shot in the head and leg, another through the thigh and the other through the side. Capt. Tilden had a bullet take the skin from his throat another had the flesh taken from the back of his head and one was slightly wounded in the hand—there I believe I have given you all the casualties of Co B. Several of the boys had air holes in their blankets while on their backs I was sorry to hear that you have not received that money yet, but I guess it will come along soon, as all through the war (ie as long as I am here). Sixteen dollars every two months will come the same as that*

*has or will—darling wife I hope that ere another summer rolls around to have the great joy of greeting you in Maine and I hope it may be with perfect health and with unimpaired limbs, then we can truly appreciate the joys of peace and domestic life and then can begin to form a home for my darling, which I should have done ere I married, had I done so you would not now of been without an abiding place...and may God protect thee will be the prayer of Wesley*

By then, Wesley was as good a soldier as any in the Union Army, but being a good soldier is no protection from Fate. Wesley's life was hastening to its end by the end of June. The Peninsula Campaign stalled short of its goal of taking Richmond and June was not a good month for the Union Army. Both Wesley and his brother George were taken prisoner at the battle of Gaines Mill on June 27. A bullet shattered George's ankle and Wesley would not leave his brother on the battlefield without care and at the mercy of vengeful Confederates. As a consequence, and after four days in the field of wondering what was going to happen to them, both were captured. George received treatment, was sent to Libby Prison in Richmond, and was released before Wesley, who spent forty days at Belle Isle Prison, also in Richmond. During the latter days of Wesley's incarceration, Sabrina wrote this letter to Luky:

*Castine July 30 1862*
*My Very dear Sister:*
*Though it has been a few days since I wrote you I think I will improve. A moment this morning in placing*

a few of my roaming thoughts on this paper! My health is quite good at present, better than it has been for some time—

Well sis, Bro Geo J Brown returned home last Saturday. He was wounded quite severely in the right leg near the ankle. A ball about the size of my thimble went in one side of his leg and was cut out on the other side, the ball passing between the two bones and slivering a piece from one of the bones. He can't stand on his foot yet.

We have had plenty of company since George returned. Some days fifty persons have called to see him during the day. Night before last there was a large party from Bangor that were going down among the Islands on a fishing excursion came in here and anchored and about nine oclock come up and gave Geo a splendid serenade with the band and then gave him three cheers. There were about a hundred of them, some soldiers that were home on furlough and some of the "Elite" of Bangor.

Last night some ladies came about ten oclock and gave him another serenade, "vocal"! Capt. Charles H Tilden left town last night to join his regt, the 16th. He is a splendid officer. Bro Geo is a very fine man. I like him very much. He is sitting by the window now and wishes to be remembered to you and all the rest of the folks that he don't know.

Wesley is exchanged. I was real sorry they were exchanged. I was in hopes they would be released on "_parole_" and then Wesley could have come home and stayed a few weeks until they had made an exchange. But never mind so "must it be". My time will come one of these days.

There is to be an excursion here from Bangor on next Wednesday and I suppose I shall go up on the boat when it goes back. I should very much like to see you but if "wishes were horses etc."

They have enlisted 14 more from this place. I believe if not they have <u>got to</u> or be <u>drafted.</u> In Boston and New York they don't think nothing of any young men who have been home lousying round, when this country is in so much peril. It matters not if they are worth 5 dol or 500,000 dols. They are looked upon <u>as low mean cowards Just what they are.</u> If <u>I</u> was an unmarried lady I wouldn't marry one of them no quicker than I would one of Jeff's negros. Would you? Say <u>no, no!</u>

Well Luky I must close. Give my love to all enquiring friends and take a good share for yourself. Be a good girl and take good care of your health and don't go out nights without putting something on your head—I will write you from Bangor. Don't let anyone see this letter nor any of my letters will you. If you ever write Joanna tell her I am <u>greatly obliged</u> to her for answering my letter—

From Sister Brina

Wesley was released from Belle Isle on August 6. Though slowly starving during incarceration, Wesley made a ring for Sabrina. He wrote to her immediately upon release despite his much-weakened state:

*Encampment 2$^{nd}$ Maine Regt.*
*Harrison's Landing, Va Aug 7$^{th}$/62*
*Dearest Brina*
*Once more I have the pleasure of penning you a few lines though I shall not write much for I do not feel like writing. I was as you know taken prisoner the 27$^{th}$ of June. I was released (or rather exchanged) the 6$^{th}$ of August. I*

*got back to the regiment at 10 o'clock. We have had rather a hard time and when I get so I can write a long letter I will tell you all about it. But we will call that one of the vicissitudes of a soldier's life and so let it pass.*

*I have not gained much flesh since I was taken prisoner, but now I am well out of it—My health is or will be good as soon as I get recruited up a little. I shall not go on duty for a few days. Darling I did expect to have the pleasure of meeting you this fall but now I do not, as it was a regular exchange of prisoners—*

*I cannot write much now but write me a good long letter as soon as you get this. I shall write a few lines to George so now good day darling. Let me know if you have received any of my allotment money if you please since the first you got. Much love to all friends and lots to Brina. Yours as ever Wesley A Brown*

*PS I send you a sample of sesech money as a relic. W
This ring I made in Belle Isle while a prisoner. If not quite large enough keep it until I get back and I will enlarge it.*

Wesley was disappointed that he was among those Union and Confederates who were exchanged rather than paroled. Parole would have been more to Wesley and Sabrina's liking. If Wesley had been paroled, he would have had to promise the Confederates that he would not fight anymore and he could have returned home. Instead, he was simply exchanged and expected to return to his regiment.

Sesech money was Confederate money but named so because it was the money that the secessionist used—those who seceded from the Union. The ring might have been made from a nail that Wesley pried from a plank, bent, and finished as well as he could. He was proud of it and hoped that Sabrina would understand its sentimental and historic value.

The tone of Wesley's next letter is pessimistic. He had hoped that he would be sent home to convalesce after his release, but it would not be so. He comes to the conclusion that he would not return home until after the war ended, if he lived that long. He hopes that he would be proved wrong, but sounds discouraged:

*Encampment 2<sup>nd</sup> Me Regt.*
*Harrison's Landing Va. Aug 8th 62*
*My Own Darling Wife*
*You have doubtless been greatly disappointed in not having the pleasure of seeing me at home this season and I have thought that I would be at home before winter but now I do not think so. If my life is spared I shall be at home as soon as the war ends but I do not expect to be at home before that time. George has told you all about how he and I was taken prisoner so I will not repeat it here. I was removed from the Tobacco Warehouse the same day that I left George at the Hospital. I went and stopped all night with him and the next day was taken to Belle Isle just above the city and stopped there until Aug 5<sup>th</sup> when we were marched to the landing where our transports were, a distance of nearly 20 miles. The night of the 5<sup>th</sup> we laid outdoors. The morning of the 6<sup>th</sup> we went on board and at ten o'clock that night we reached the regt. George has told you how we fared after we got into Belle Isle. It was the same as in the Warehouses...I laid outdoors as all the tents were full when I got there.*

*We got hard fare and rough treatment while prisoners, and I hope I shall never be taken again—my health is good only I am weak from the effects of my fare while in Richmond but after a week or so I shall be well as ever ready for duty.*

*I felt disappointed when I got back to find that all the vacancies had been filled as the Capt did not expect that I should come back to the regt so I am still a private and liable to be as long as the war lasts but it is just my luck to be so and I suppose Brina will say, "Well darling all is for the best." Had I not been taken prisoner I stood a good chance for a commission before three months, but now it is as it is. Well we will let it pass.*

*Have you yet paid all your debts on the Island…have you received any money of my allotment yet, besides what you got before you left the Island. Do you think of stopping with Emma this winter—I wrote to you yesterday and sent a ring that I made while on Belle Isle. It was a poor thing but I thought you might be pleased with it as I made it while a Prisoner. I also sent some of the money such as they have in Dixie thinking you might wish to see some of it. Please to keep it as a relic—*

*I think you had better stop with Emma until I get back, unless you prefer to stop with your friends in Connecticut. I want you to write me how you first heard of my being a Prisoner and all about it if you please. When you write to Luky send my love and tell her to write to me. My love to all friends and my hearts best love to Brina. Oh darling if I could have the pleasure of pressing your loved form to my breast and smothering you with warm and thrilling kisses and feel your cheek on mine once more I should be indeed happy but that pleasure is denied me until our*

*loved Country is once more free from danger. Then, dearest, we will enjoy all the comforts of domestic life in peace and security, not again to be parted. The only thing that troubles me is not being able to send you more money than what I do but I cannot do different. So darling do the best you can and take good care of your precious self and believe me as ever your loving husband.*
    *Wesley A. Brown*

A part of a letter Brina sent to Luky was devoted to Wesley's experience in Belle Isle:

*...Wesley has arrived back to the regt. And I have received two letters from him. He was exchanged the 6$^{th}$ of this month, he suffered very much while a prisoner. Everything was impure from the stench of the dead and dying and all eatables were exceedingly high. Wesley with his "Mess" which is about ten men sold a watch and bought a barrel of flour and paid 25 dollars for it, and sold enough besides their rations from that barrel to buy another for which they paid 23 dollars. They had no salt for the reason that they couldn't get it at any price. It was 28 dollars per bushel and none at that molasses 8 dols per gal. Calico shirts 7.50 per piece. Everything to wear and everything to eat is just so high and little to be had at that price. It is my opinion that they will have to "Skeedaddle" unless they receive help from some other nation soon—I would write you a great deal about them that bro George has told me, but I have not time nor space. Wesley sent much love to you so write to him as soon as you could and you will please do so. I will enclose you his address. The 18$^{th}$ Regt leaves here next week. I am going to see them and I*

*wished you was here to see them too. They are encamped about two miles from here and this PM they have a sermon to them from one of the clergy of Bangor. It is at 5 o'clock.*

*I am at Uncle Cyrus's now. It is very pleasant here and I like it very much. They are all very kind and pleasant and live in fine style at the corner of French and Sommerset Streets. I expect to stay here four or five weeks and will write you quite often. Give my love to all and lots to Luky.
From Brina*

Wesley admired the competent and sober officers in his company, especially Capt. Tilden of Castine. Though he wanted to be an officer, Wesley was not able to advocate for himself like successful candidates apparently did. As a result, he was jealous of and bitter toward men who became officers even though he believed he was better qualified. He was a prisoner in Richmond when there was a round of promotions, but nobody expected him to return from incarceration so he was passed over. It would have pleased Wesley to send more money home because, in his own mind, it would have strengthened his role as provider to his island wife, but after return from incarceration, he abandoned hope of being promoted. Had he survived Second Manassas, he probably would have stood a good chance of advancing rank to replace an officer killed in that battle.

The last letter that Wesley sent to Sabrina before he was wounded at Second Manassas was written at Fredericksburg while the Second Maine was in the Fifth Corps under General Porter and, ultimately, General Pope. Wesley would be fatally wounded in a week and he had a

little more than a month to live:
> Fredericksburg Va Aug 22/62
> Headquarters 2$^{nd}$ Me Regt
> My Own darling Brina
> Again I will try to pen a few lines knowing that they would be welcomed by you. For the past week I have been anxiously expecting a letter from you but as yet none have come from Brina since I returned from my premature visit to Richmond which did not please me very well, as you will probably believe when you read my letters of the 7$^{th}$, 8$^{th}$ and 10$^{th}$ which I wrote soon after my return while at Harrison's Landing—
> On the night of the 14$^{th}$ we left Harrison's Landing and marched twenty-six miles before the next night, when we stopped over night at the mouth of the Chickehoming and the next morning started and marched about 17 miles and then stopped for the night at Williamsburg, the scene of one of the victories of the Union arms. The next day we went to Yorktown, a distance of 19 miles and bivouacked on our old camping ground that we had at the siege—
> But I must stop for the mail is going. I am well and so is all friends. Much love to all friends. Tell George I would write if I had the time. With much love. I am yours as ever.
>   Wesley
>   PS Lots of kisses for Brina and all my heart's best love.
>   Wesley

Sabrina wrote a long letter on August 14, which may or may not have reached him before the battle of Second Manassas. We can only hope it did, but when an army is on the move, the mail might not be as predictable as it is when there is a lull in the fighting. Though it may seem as if Wesley would have read it—it was retrieved among his other belongings at the hospital after he died—he claims in his very last letter, dated September 6, that he hadn't heard from Sabrina since he was taken prisoner. It would seem more likely than not that he did read it or that it was read to him by a nurse or friend when the letter finally found him, but his comment on September 6 only the perpetuates the mystery.

Sabrina's letter was written in response to one of the several letters Wesley wrote to her at Harrison's Landing. It was a very good letter—long, sensitive and sympathetic:

*Castine Aug 14/1862*
*My very dear Wesley*

*I was made very happy tonight by receiving your kind and most heart-cheering letter. Yes, darling, I was exceedingly glad to receive that precious letter. I was so thankful that you got away from that horrible sesech kingdom but, really, I prayed that you might be released on parole for I thought then perhaps that I should have the inexpressible pleasure of greeting you so warmly at Home. It made me feel quite melancholy when George came home though I felt glad for him and Emma too she was so glad and happy. I could but rejoice for her. But dearest I am grateful to think that you are still alive and I hope that by this time that your health is good as can be expected.*

*For a time I really looked for you at home and used to watch the Packet and stage as much as though I had rec'd a direct dispatch from you to that effect. Never mind. Brina will wait. She can do that can't she dearest precious Wesley, but O, I want to see you so much, how much words are inadequate to describe and it seems kind of hard. But after all this there is a time coming is there not dearest. And I know of someone who can look beyond the gloomy present to a bright and joyous future which I trust may in a measure compensate for the dark and shady past. I know you must have fared outrageously there at Richmond and I think it perfectly horrid. George told me something about it so I have something of an idea about Richmond in general. But enough of that for I should judge that the very sound of Richmond would be loathsome to anyone that had passed any time within the walls. Well, dearest, at the present I am the only person that is up in the house, all having retired. Geo finished writing to you some time ago and absconded and Alice followed suit so my dear you see that I am left all alone to have a fine silent chat with you. And I presume you won't be particular what I write so long as I am not too sober or sour or rather cross. And as I feel neither very sour nor very sober you may expect something a little between.*

*Perhaps you would like to know how I like the society of my new bro—very much indeed, I answer, most readily. I think he is very kind and Emma seems so happy, and it makes me feel so glad to see her happy and enjoying herself. But one of these days Brina will be happy too, won't I darling at least if I'm not it will be my own fault for I know if I could live always near you and had my health I would not envy Queen Victoria. Do you believe it—*

*Dearest I read the note which you wrote to George and I thought by its tone that you didn't feel in very good spirits and was rather disappointed in not being promoted. Never mind dear soljer boy. It is better to merit promotion* and not have it (as I know you do) than to have it and not merit it as do two-thirds of the army officers. Capt Or rather Col. Tilden complimented you very highly here in Castine. I thought he is a very fine man. He said he wished he could see you. He would give your hand one good shaking. He seemed to think a vast deal of you and Brina does too so don't look so sober and lose all the flesh you have in consequence will you darling because Brina loves you just as well as she ever did and that is saying considerable and a vast deal better don't you think, I do.

You come home and see if I don't. That's a darling precious husband. I send a thousand kisses and bright wishes for your dear self but if you was only here your face would smart for one long time, all night anyhow. O dearest if it was only you instead of Ally that I was going to sleep with tonight how very glad I would be. But then Brina will be very patient and a very good girl until Wesley comes home. I will finish this on the outside of George's letter. I am very much obliged for that cunning ring. It is plenty large for my little finger.

We hope that that ring is in the possession of a descendant of Sabrina's or that it is housed in a museum somewhere and that there is someone who knows its history and value as a symbol of a marriage besieged by war and sustained by the mail, until death brought the correspondence to an end.

# SECOND MANASSAS: THE COURT OF DEATH

The "bright and joyous future" was not to be. Wesley's luck ran out at the battle of Second Manassas between August 28 and August 30, 1862, one of many pre-Gettysburg battles that took place in the region around Washington and Richmond. Wesley Brown and the Second Maine were among about sixty-two thousand other Union soldiers under General Pope. Pope's army was then near the site of the first battle of the Civil War, fought thirteen months earlier, called First Manassas by Southerners, who won that battle and so have a kind of authority over the name. Northerners called First Manassas "First Bull Run," after the stream named Bull Run that flows through the area. Pope's soldiers entered the area in pursuit of "Stonewall" Jackson, one of General Lee's two top commanders, the other being Longstreet, who was on his way to join Jackson in a combined effort to pursue and annihilate Pope before the Federal forces under McClellan arrived in the area.

By that time, the Confederates had successfully defended Richmond and were seeking a fight that would cripple the Union Army and make Washington, D.C., vulnerable. After the battle at Cedar Mountain on August 9, a battle which Wesley missed, Lee had hoped to trap Pope, but Pope received intelligence that warned him about Lee's plan so he withdrew to the east side of the Rappahannock, where he and Lee skirmished between August 22 and 25. Wesley had caught up with the army by then, though it's hard to imagine that he was fully recovered from the hardships of incarceration.

Lee had a pretty good idea he could destroy Pope's army, so he sent Stuart behind Pope to cut off the latter's communications with Washington, D.C., and he sent Jackson north to raid, sack, and destroy Pope's supplies at Manassas Junction. Thinking he was clever enough and strong enough to destroy Jackson, Pope withdrew from the Rappahannock and headed north as quickly as he could. Not only did he want to fight Jackson, but he knew that Washington, D.C., was now vulnerable. The location of the battle was where Jackson hoped it would be—around the vicinity of Groveton, Virginia, where First Manassas was fought. Lee was eager to destroy Pope before McCellan arrived, and Pope wanted to destroy Jackson before Longstreet arrived. So Wesley Brown's last battle would be in the same place as his first. He would barely survive the battle, but not the wound he received there.

# TIMETABLE TO HELL

Among the letters in Wesley's file at the Islesboro Historical Society is a single sheet of paper that has entries written on it as if it were a diary. These entries count down the days between Wesley's release from Belle Isle and his arrival at Groveton, Virginia, where First and Second Manassas were fought:

*Aug 1$^{st}$ Pleasant on Belle Isle. Hungry.*
*Aug 2$^{nd}$ ditto*
*Aug 3$^{rd}$ ditto*
*Aug 4$^{th}$ The same.*
*Aug 5$^{th}$ Was up all night having our names taken down. Today we marched twenty miles to our boats.*
*Aug 6$^{th}$ Stopped in a field on the bend of the river last night and went on board the boats. Went down river and joined our regts tonight.*
*Aug 7 Have been writing all day to friends and living high.*
*Aug 8 ditto*
*Aug 9 The same.*
*Aug 11 Hot and sultry. All the sick sent off.*
*Aug 12 ditto*
*Aug 13 Still warm. Col. Varney and Mudgett and Capt Emmerson got back from Richmond today.*
*Aug 14 Heat. Still waiting to march.*
*Aug 15 On the march down river. Crossed the Chickhominy at dark.*
*Aug 16 Marched from the mouth of the Chickhominy to Williamsburgh. Camped on the old battlefield.*

*17 Marched to Yorktown and camped on the ground we used to occupy.*

*18 Marched to Hampton today*

*19th Went to Newport News and went off boat.*

*Aug 20th Went down to Fortress Monroe today. Start up the bay at noon.*

*Aug 21st Got to Agnew Creek and land. Go on the cars to Fredericksburg.*

*Aug 22 Start at dark on the march.*

*Aug 23 Marched all last night and all day. At night we are near some miles about twenty miles from Fredericksburg. Lost my diary today. Was very sick last night.*

*Aug 24 Cloudy today. For the past week it has been hot and sultry. Are now under marching orders. Started at noon and went about eight miles. Camped for the night.*

*Aug 25 Pleasant and warm. Struck tents and marched into the road and then back again and settled down for the night.*

*Aug 26 Hot and sultry. Marched twenty miles today. No meat for three days.*

*Aug 27 Heat. Marched twenty miles today. Was at battle fought at Manassas—*

*Aug 28 Pleasant but hot and sultry. Marched ten miles today. Are near the battleground of yesterday. Have had nothing to eat today but a few hard breads. Went and had a good wash.*

These brief entries track Wesley's last days before he was mortally wounded during intense fighting at Groveton. There, the bullet that was molded for Wesley Brown would enter its fated target, exit, and fall to the ground a distance away, soaked with blood and flecked with minute pieces of gore.

Jackson arrived at Groveton before Pope and was well prepared for the arrival of Union forces. He positioned his men in a long, wide, man-made trench—an unfinished railroad bed excavation called a cut. Gravel banks rose on either side of the cut. These banks were at least as tall as a man and they provided excellent cover for the Confederates as they repelled Union charges. This unfinished railroad bed is a curious sort of symbol of the carnage at Second Manassas. It resembled a long, open grave waiting to be filled.

Second Manassas was a three-day engagement between Pope's army and the combined forces of Longstreet and Jackson under Lee. Dusk on the end of the third day saw Pope's mangled Union Army in a desperate but professional and orderly—maybe even heroic—retreat across a stone bridge that spanned Bull Run. If the railroad cut resembled a long, open grave then the Warrenton Turnpike was just its opposite: a life-giving artery providing the bloodied remnant of Pope's army a way out of the threat of annihilation by Longstreet, Jackson, and Lee.

The survivors of Jackson's tenacity, Pope's presumptuousness, and Longstreet's artillery and devastating charge would regroup at Centerville, east of Groveton, where Pope should have gone to wait for McClellan before he undertook to attack Jackson. Even so, the survivors of Second Manassas would, with the support of reinforcements, repel an attack by Jackson's pursuing army at the battle of Chantilly on September 1. On the third day of that three-day engagement at Groveton, Wesley Brown was wounded and, in a month, in his bed in the Baptist Hospital in Alexandria, his wound would kill him.

Imagination is the mother of empathy. One can imagine the carnage that occurred during the fight along the railroad embankments, where Wesley might have been wounded, and so one can empathize with the suffering of someone as seriously injured as he was. If we couldn't empathize with the suffering of those who have lost a limb, an eye, or even a mind in battle, or with the suffering of spouses who lose their loved ones, then war would become something that we no longer sought to prevent. We would pursue it like we would a thrill and we would turn our faces from the maimed, ignore the dead, and avoid the grieving.

During the three-day engagement, the 2nd Maine Volunteer Regiment was in General Porter's Fifth Corps. Major Daniel Sargent led the regiment during Porter's assault against the railroad cut, where, on August 30, Jackson's soldiers were still well entrenched. Since the 2nd Maine was in the worst of the fighting at Second Manassas, and since he was wounded on the thirtieth, it may very well be that Wesley was shot at or near the unfinished railroad bed. He would have seen astounding suffering. Not only were Union soldiers fully exposed to Jackson's musket fire in front of them, but they were exposed to Longstreet's artillery as well, off to their left as they charged. Pope stopped sending soldiers into this deathtrap only after Longstreet's infantry charged the mass of bloodied bluecoats, forcing Pope to abandon his stubborn quest to destroy Jackson and save his own army instead.

Well-organized and self-sacrificing Union resistance

on higher ground allowed the Federals time to retreat across Manassas plain and over Bull Run, but Wesley was left behind on the battlefield.

A description of Wesley's wound and the amount of time he spent unattended on the field are recorded in Sabrina's September 18 letter to sister, Luky:

*Well, Luky, I have heard from Wesley. I rec'd a letter last Saturday night. He was very severely wounded on the 30th of Aug—the ball passing entirely through the lower part of his body. He said it was very miraculous that it didn't instantly kill him, and would surely have done so had the ball entered one inch higher or one inch to one side, and was fearful that it might terminate in death now, but he said he didn't mean it should, he lay on the field 48 hours after he fell, and then was picked up and put in an ambulance, and rode fifty miles over a Virginia road which no example in the state of Maine will equal, so that it was 104 hours after he was wounded before he had his wound dressed or tasted anything to eat or drink! Don't you think that was <u>horrid!</u> He was entirely helpless, couldn't turn, sit nor stand, but he never murmured once, only saying that he had met with the fate of a "soldier". He wrote nothing about how he suffered, but he wrote his bros. and I read the letter. He wrote me that his wound was "doing well", but said he wouldn't be able to <u>move</u> for a month, poor fellow. How bad it makes me feel. I should like to go and take care of him if they allow me to, but his folks don't think I had better as I could not be with him much after I got out there, and perhaps it would not pay after all.*

The location of the wound suggests that Wesley was shot at very close range because the course of the ball passed so close to the centerline of his body. There is a strong possibility, then, that Wesley was very close to the Confederate guns at the railroad excavation and that Confederates held their fire until charging Union soldiers were quite near, in order not to waste ammunition. This is probably why the ball passed through him. Though we have no pictures of Wesley Brown, any picture that illustrates any Union soldier in action on the gravel banks of the unfinished railroad bed at Second Manassas might as well be an artist's illustration of Private Wesley Brown moments before he fell.

And after he fell, the Federals retreated, leaving Wesley on the battlefield—not alone because hundreds of other Federals and Confederates, dead and wounded, lay close by. At least the dead are quiet. We can only imagine the weeping and howls of the injured and dying as Wesley clutched his wound, probably lying on his side with his legs drawn up, not moving, not murmuring, for two days. We need also to keep in mind that Pope's soldiers ate hardly at all during the three-day engagement because Jackson looted and burned their supplies the day before the battle began, and Wesley was still recovering from the deprivations of incarceration. Wesley fell on August 30. On September 1, two days later, and after he was loaded onto a horse-drawn ambulance, he probably heard the sound of battle again, at Chantilly, near Centerville, as he rode the ambulance down the Warrenton Turnpike toward the capital. It rained heavily that night.

Wesley was taken to the Baptist Church Hospital on Washington Street in Alexandria, Virginia. The hospital was an active Baptist church until three months earlier when a Union Army guard unit occupied the building during a worship service and converted the space for use as a hospital for Union wounded. The bapistry—a large tub used for total immersion baptisms—was used for washing wounded soldiers. It was there that Wesley wrote this short letter to his island wife, the last letter he was able to write with his own hand:

*Baptist Church Hospital Alexandria Sept 6th*
*Dear Brina,*
*I have at last met with a soldier's fate but fortunately I guess I will recover and then peace and quiet with my Brina at home. I am very weak but my wound is going well. I have not as yet heard from you since I went to Richmond—I shall not be able to know for a month yet, write to me as soon as you get this. I wrote to you about sending a diary.*

Sabrina must have been stunned to read that Wesley received none of her letters since he was prisoner. Despite her best efforts and repeated mailings, not a letter was getting through. Wesley didn't know that Sabrina worried a great deal about him. Just when he needed her the most, and she was trying her hardest to make mutual contact, the mail seemed to function at its worst.

*Bangor September 3 1862*
*Dear Sister... I have heard the painful intelligence of my dear Wesley's being wounded and in the hospital. I haven't heard any of the particulars only that he is wounded in the hip. I fear it will prove very serious but I*

*have very very much to be thankful for. I don't know how badly he is wounded. But it's being in the hip so I fear it is a serious wound and it's very gratifying to me to know that he is not a prisoner and that his name is not among the killed of the recent great and horrid battles. O Luky you don't know anything about it. I hear two or three times every day from the seat of war. The loss of the 2$^{nd}$ Maine in the recent battle is 75, it was reported, that Col. Roberts was killed but now it is contradicted. I am going down to the Hall this afternoon to work for the Soldiers...*

Sabrina was hearing the first news of Second Manassas and she was frustrated with conflicting reports, especially reports about who died. She couldn't trust the reliability of the news she was receiving two or three times a day. Wesley's wound was in his abdomen and back, not his hip, and the wound had already been diagnosed on the field as being untreatable, but Sabrina didn't know that. She decided to go to the Hall so she could divert her mind from thinking about the worst that might have happened and so she could feel as if her work would benefit the soldiers—and Wesley—somehow.

Here is the second letter from Wesley, written by an attendant as he lay on his bed in the Baptist Church Hospital, Alexandria, Virginia:

*PS Direct as below and enclose pocket handkerchief*
*Washington St Baptist Church Hospital, Alexandria, Sept 11 '62*
*Dear Brina*
*Through the kindness of my attendant I will write you a few lines to inform you that I am getting along comfort-*

*ably. Although my four limbs are still my own and will remain so, yet being compelled by my wound to lie down most of the time. It is very difficult for me to write you except through my attendant. Our hospital is situated on the most aristocratic street in Alexandria and so far as I can learn is the pleasantest one in the city. A few days ago a lot of Boston boys came out here to act as nurses and one of them writes as I dictate. Now my dear wife, don't worry in the least but remain strong in the belief that you will again see your husband in as sound a condition as when he left you. We have one or two Maine boys among the wounded and one of them, a Captain, has now with him his wife and child. I doubt if they add at all to his physical comfort and most certainly it must be very unpleasant for them. Although the sight of my wife's face would make me jump with joy—yet I wouldn't for the world have you here. In fact the pleasure of seeing you on my return will be all the greater from having passed through the hospital without your being present to witness the sufferings of some of the patients more severely wounded than myself.*

*Patients here find good care and skilful surgeons. For my own part no surgical operations has been necessary—I need only to have my wound washed and dressed and then I can read, talk, and <u>think</u> of you. Our regt is at Fort Corcoran. I recd ten letters from home yesterday and enjoyed a rich treat. Whenever I want fruit I send out and get it and every day chicken soup and cakes and flowers are brought in in any quantity by the ladies of this city. Now Brina dear if I don't receive two letters a week from you regularly I will never come home until I have been through a course of gymnastics training that will make me strong enough to give you the hardest shaking that* you ever recd in all the days of your life. More in my next. And now listen still for a moment. It is raining here and but one thought but troubles me and that is that it is also rains where you are and that you are getting your dress wet. Give my love to all the Bangor folks and ask them to write. Yr affectionate husband W.A. Brown

No surgical operations had been necessary because the army medical staff knew that all they could do was clean and change Wesley's dressings and pray that the wound would heal. On September 14, gangrene set in and Wesley and his attendant knew that his death would follow within days. Wesley said that there would be "more in my next" but there would be no "next," only a letter from his attendant informing Sabrina of Wesley's death.

It was during Wesley's decline that his sister-in-law Minta, Charles Brown's wife, wrote an urgent letter to Sabrina. Minta was of two minds. She would write as if Wesley were already dead, but she also wrote as if there were hope that he would recover. For the time, it was an appropriate perspective because Wesley died the day after Minta wrote the letter and while the letter was in transit to Sabrina.

*Bangor Sept 22 1862*
*My Dear Sister*

*What can I say to you in this hour of great trouble. I fear that our late news is too true. O Wesley, Thou art an idolized son, an adored husband and a near and dear brother. Noble self-sacrificing young man! O must thou this early bid a \_\_\_\_ to earth. Must we can see past with you. O Brina I fear that I shall fail to say anything comforting but I know I feel deeply for you. My first words* *on receiving the dispatch was poor Brina and then poor Mother, poor Charles and George. True we can none of us feel as you do. O that my pen could indict some supporting words to your bereaved heart. Yes yes there is comfort and consolation when we look on the right side and think that our loss is his gain. How great his gain, when he exchanges this world of sin, toil and strife for that blessed abode of peace among the blessed. I feel that dying grace will be his. Only think of that letter written after he was wounded, never murmured or complained, never mentioned his great sufferings. O it seemed to me so Christlike that I have since felt at times that God was about to take one so lovely to himself. The Lord giveth and the Lord taketh away. Blessed is the name of the Lord. Charles says we can not give him up. He thinks there is a chance for hope and says tell Brina she need not thus give Wesley up. He may take a favorable turn yet and God grant it may be so. Dear Sister you have many sympathizing friends here but we have all got to bear our own burdens. Let us try and be prepared for the worst. Let us try and feel and say Father thy will not mine be done. O Wesley was very near and dear to me. Many were the pleasing and high prospects I had in store for him. My poor heart is sadly torn yet I have much to live for. But O if Wesley goes before it will certainly greatly ween us all from earth.*

*Dear little Ida says Mother what makes you look so poor and sick. When I told her she cried and sobbing says we shall never see Uncle Wesley in this world but we shall in another and if we pray God will take care of him. That said in childish simplicity was quite comforting to me and she says how bad aunt Brina will feel. But she would feel worse if it was her father and taking it to herself she sobbed a long while, then says O Mother I can't take any comfort here. May I not go to Mrs. Nourses. I take good comfort there. Mrs. Nourse don't cry as you do. Poor child. I tried hard to be more cheerful. But O it was very affecting to hear her say her prayer. O God take care of uncle Wesley (who can't live but a short time) give him a holy heart and take him into heaven and then O God take care of aunt Brina and give her a holy heart to love God. O my dear Sister God will sustain you and you will be yet the means of doing great good in the world.*

*O it is a great honor to die thus, uncomplaining for his country. More honor than if he was put in command of our whole army. And yet there is hope that he may stay with us and endure yet a little longer the storm and bustle of this sinful world. O Thou giver of good and perfect gifts, if it be thy will, spare O spare that loved one, to cheer the lone path of his darling companion, orphan as she is, take not away this early her all on earth. Thy will, not mine, be done. Mrs. Nourse send you her love and sympathy.*

*Now dear Sister I have written you a broken epistle full of grief sprinkled in with a little hope. What may be our next news God only knows. Let it come. This is painful anxiety. I will return those dear lines enclosed in your letter. You were very good to write us when your trouble was so great. And O if we could do anything for you. Let us hear again, come yourself when you can feel to. Lean on us all you can and be sure of support as far as we have strength.*

*Now much love from Minta*

*Where is George why is he not with Wesley*

Finally, the expected and dreaded letter came: *Alexandria, Va*

*Sept. 24$^{th}$ 62*

*Mrs. Wesley Brown
Dear Madame*
*Two weeks ago last Saturday evening I reached this hospital, being one of a party sent out to act as nurses to the wounded. Among the patients in my ward I found a young man whose fine face and pleasant manners immediately attracted my attention. Several times each day it was my duty to dress his wound. We soon became intimate and from his own lips I learned the particulars of the 2$^{nd}$ fight at Bull Run, in which he received his dreadful wound. An order was given to Wesley's company which, owing to the noise of the battle, the officers failed to hear. Your husband, however, having been more fortunate in hearing the order repeated it to the men and turning to see if they were obeying it, received a ball about 2 inches to the left of the bottom of the spine. The bullet passed completely through the body coming out a little below and to the left of the navel. A surgeon on the battlefield told him that nothing could be done, the wound was mortal. He lay thus wounded 48 hours without attention, was then placed on an ambulance, from which, after a ride of 52 hours, he was taken out at this place. Our surgeon said nothing concerning the wound calculated to alarm, whether from motives of prudence, or from a belief that it was not fatal. I do not know. For my own part, wholly inexperienced in such matters, I had scarcely an opinion. I think Wesley regarded his cure as very probable. At any rate he kept up the best of spirits, had a capital appetite, digested his food, read a great deal and seemed happy. Such was condition at the time I wrote, to his dictation, a letter to you containing one to your brother-in-law*

*Lieut Brown. In a few days, appearances changed, and on Sunday, 14th, instead it was evident that mortification had set in. Your husband fully realized his condition and began to dictate some farewell letters, but finally decided to leave the matter with me, believing, as he did, that death would be immediate. Thinking the same myself I thought also that information of his sad condition would not reach you until it would be too late for you to reach this city until some days after his death and burial. But to my great surprise he lingered along until Tuesday 16th when I forwarded a note to Lieut Brown regarding then to state the circumstances. Still he lingered until yesterday, Tuesday 23rd between 5 and 6 P.M. when he died. His mother and sister were written to as soon as symptoms became fatal and I shall write again informing them of his death. He left in money three dollars forty-nine cents which I enclose. His testament, knife, glass etc. are here and if not called for by Lieut Brown will reach you in time. His diary was lost in the battle. I will not attempt to condole with you in your grief. The worth of such a husband is too well known and his loss too deeply felt to admit of any consolation from such as I.*

*I am respectfully C. Edward Cram*
*Baptist Church Hospital*

In several letters of the correspondence, Wesley had complained that he was being overlooked for an officer's commission. He didn't want to remain a private. Ironically, the one time when he was fully prepared to act like an officer in the thick of battle, to relay an officer's order to the men and then observe the results of that order, he was shot. We don't know what effect that order had on the progress of the fight. We can only hope that Wesley's sacrifice helped the Union that day.

Mr. Cram wrote that Wesley's 1862 diary was lost in the battle. But Wesley wrote in his single-sheet "timetable" that he lost his diary on August 23, during the march to Manassas and not during any battle. Though small, this discrepancy is curious. Both explanations for the loss of Wesley's diary can't be true because the loss couldn't have happened in two different places. It seems most likely that Wesley lost his diary on the march because he recorded the event while it happened and when he was fit enough to take inventory of his belongings.

Such seemingly small details like this are important when tracking a man's last days, especially when the act of writing sustained his marriage and his humanity, and provided him a perspective on the historic, national drama in which he knew he was playing a role.

Though Brina might have written more letters after the one dated September 13, those letters are not in the collection. As far as it is known, the following letter is Brina's last to Wesley:

*Bangor Sept. 13, 1862 My Dear and Cherished Wesley*
*It is with feelings of the deepest gratitude that I attempt to address a few lines to you, the dearest to me of earthly objects. Darling you cannot imagine how very thankful I am to receive your precious note of the 6th—it being the first reliable news I have received from you since that terrible battle or from any source and you may well believe that your letter was perused with as grateful feelings as my anxious heart was ever the author of. My let-*

ter was remailed in Castine and also the one you wrote to Geo. He not being at home. He left here for the seat of war last Thursday and was going to see if he could find you. I wrote a letter to you and sent it by him. I have also written you about a half a dozen and sent them by mail but I don't presume you will ever receive either one of them.

Darling the letter you wrote George was thrilling indeed. O can it be possible that you have suffered so cruelly. O it comes so hard. You was not going to tell Brina anything about your suffering so severely was you, but I read that letter so it didn't matter if you didn't write me. I wish it was in my power to care of you. I should be so happy if I could. It would be such a pleasant task to watch with you all night and to hold and bathe your precious and weary head. I wished you was here, or I was with you. Though it would pain me to see you suffering yet I should know to what extent you suffered and would be so tender of you. O I know that none could nurse you more tenderly and none could anticipate your every wish more readily than I. Do you think they could darling, and don't you wish you was here. O I do. And I am sincere in saying so. But I will patiently wait putting my trust in "him" who doeth all for the best though he works in a mysterious way. But I must affirm that I think that it was through "Divine" aid that your dear life was spared and I shall never cease to be grateful for his kind and watchful care over you. And again I will not soon cease to cherish any animosity which is everyday strengthening and maturing against this distracted and decomposed government. So much political strife and office-seeking, so many ill-timed, ill-contrived, ill maneuvered and non-victorious conflicts. The origin of their ill succor/success being in the shortsightedness of our "leading men". Generally there has been suffering sufficient already to *have saved a nation if it had only been "well timed". It does distress me to think of it and for you suffering long without any assistance seems almost intolerable. It will disgrace the pages of American history. I have read of our soldiers being left to suffer that length of time before but Heaven knows that it never came quite so near before though I have always viewed it as unjust and needless suffering—as many good surgeons as we have it seems so cruel instead—Hope says that it is darkest before day. Yes but O what a dark night. No moon, no stars. I hope George has been to see you ere this for I know that you will be glad to see him. Direct your next to Castine and tell me if I can send you anything and I will do so—I hope dearest that you will excuse this letter and forgive if I have said aught too much—dearest how can I help it when you have endured so much suffering with thousands of others and all; I was going to say "for nothing". The majority of people here are losing all confidence in Government—But darling I will stop for I may make your brain more weary by my idle talk. Goodby… May kind heaven tenderly guard every moment of your life is the earnest prayer of* **Brina**

*Wesley write me just as often as you can if no more than a line so I can know how you get along and come home as soon as you are able to be moved so I can take care of you myself on my own bed. Bless your life how I love you dear precious sufferer. Keep up good courage my darling and O don't _____ and leave Brina all alone! You will come north won't you dearest—they all send much love to you. From Brina*

Sabrina did not want to write the word "die" in her plea at the closing of the letter, presumably because she feared it would jinx Wesley's chances of recovery. We need to remember that Sabrina lost three parents and a brother while she was very young. Within four years, she would lose her oldest brother, Robert Nelson, and her sister, Luky. To lose a husband then would perpetuate a cycle of grief. She wrote the letter the day before Wesley knew that his wound was mortal—but well before he died—so he probably had the opportunity to have it read to him by his attendant. He died on September 23, ten days after the date of Sabrina's letter. We know that he received her last letter because it was among those things that were retrieved by Wesley's brother. Unless he was unconscious after the letter arrived, Wesley died knowing that at least his letters were reaching Sabrina and that his wife still loved him.

Though the bodies of many Union soldiers were returned home and buried by their families, Wesley's body was not. Sometimes financial considerations determined whether or not a body would be shipped north. Wesley's body was removed from the Baptist Church Hospital and was buried in a new cemetery in Alexandria reserved for Union soldiers. Sabrina's letters to Wesley were sent to her by Wesley's brother George, who visited the hospital during his return south to his regiment after a period of convalescence with his wife, Emma, in Castine. He had hoped to visit Wesley at the Baptist Church Hospital in Alexandria on his way back to duty, but Wesley died before George arrived. There was little George could do except visit his brother's grave and send Wesley's few remaining items—including several of Sabrina's letters—back home. From Annapolis, Maryland, George wrote a letter to Sabrina:

*My dear Sister Brina,*

*I have just returned from Alexandria. I found the Baptist Church Hospital and Brother's things. They are not of much amount but I will send them to you by express. I got all the things he had when there. He lost his diary on the battlefield. I found where he was buried and visited his grave. He is buried in what is called the New Burying Ground or the Soldiers New Ground. He was buried as well as he could have been buried at home. It was a very pretty place and there is a headboard to his grave with this on it: W.A. Brown Co. B 2<sup>nd</sup> Maine Vols. As soon as I see his grave to see how well he was cared for I felt much better. I saw them bury one man while I was there and he was buried in nice shape. There are a number of officers in the same line of Graves with Wesley. I can send and have him taken up at any time by sending to Dr. Holmes, Alexandria. It will cost $15.00 to have him sent home. I will write to Dr. Holmes of Alexandria and find out what he will charge to send him home now or next winter. I should of sent him home when I was in Alexandria if I had the money but I have not got enough to pay my bills until I get paid off again. You will please see what Charles says about it and inform me at once. I am very sorry that I did not get that letter that was sent soon after I left home for I could of seen Brother before he left the farm. Oh if only I could have seen him. How much better I should have felt. But sister he is among those who are happy so cheer up. God saw fit to call him away and there was no hope of his living after he was shot. He was a noble and brave man and the Army has lost a brave soldier as it ever had and he could not have fallen for a better cause. So do not mourn nor be sad for he may be near thee always and if you are sad then he will be so to. I feel that I shall yet hear from* *him or that he is happy etc It may be my lot to Fall soon either in Battle or by fever and I feel that I cannot die in a more noble cause than Fighting for my Country.*

*You may think that the lines on this page are strange but time will tell. I am very sorry that you have lost such a good husband. You did not live with him but a short time so you cannot know so much about him as I think I do of his goodness. Well, dear sister, look on the bright side for it cannot be helped.*

*I will send a knife to Emma that I had in my trunk with your things by express. Well goodby sister. I must write a line to Emma and Charles. So good by—*
    *Your affectionate Brother*
    *George*

It may be because Wesley was buried as well as he could have been at home that his family decided to leave his body buried in New Burying Ground, now called the Alexandria National Cemetery. Sabrina might have been comforted by what George said about Wesley's grave being in the same row as the graves of officers. It was nice of George to say that. At least a couple of times, Wesley expressed his desire to become an officer and, ironically, he died while believing that he was acting like one. George searches for appropriate words that might provide Sabrina some comfort, calling forth a patriotic theme and praising Wesley's inherent goodness. Despite these sincere efforts, Sabrina was right when she said what she did when her husband left the island fifteen months earlier, and those same words suit the occasion of hearing of her husband's death: "No one knows the sorrow of that hour except those who experience it."

# WIDOWHOOD

We make legends of the dead by remembering those things that shed a good and sometimes holy light on their lives. Wesley's mother wrote a letter of consolation to Brina soon after she received word of her son's death. In it we learn that when Wesley was eleven, he and a friend were praying in the woods, and there and then they were reborn in Christ. Their story ignited a local religious revival. As a consequence, the local Baptist church welcomed many new members. Wesley's mother proudly recalls how her son reversed the town's fall into sinful ways:

*Monticello*
  *October 12, 1862*

*My dear child,*
  *What can I say to you in this trying hour for I feel that I too have met with great loss. Then we will mingle our tears together for he was dear to us both. When I heard that my darling boy was dangerously wounded I felt that all my hopes were blasted and my expectations were cut off for I always thought if I should live to be old he would be the one that I should live with. He was always a noble child. I never known him to tell a lie in any way. Try to envision me when Wesley was eleven years old. We lived in Belmont, Me, it was a time of general declination in religion. There was no meetings held in the place and Wesley used to feel that it was not right many would get together and play cards. Wesley and another boy that lived near agreed together to get religion unbeknown to any of their*

*friends and one Sunday they went into the woods and prayed all day and when they came home they were happy and said they found the savior and from that time there was a great reformation and it spread all through the town. Wesley was baptized and many others and joined the Free Will Baptist church in Belmont. I have hopes that he did not forget to pray amid the din of war. He wrote me last winter that there was hardly a day but what he read from the sacred pages of the Bible. I hope my dear Child that it will be a consolation to you to know that our beloved Wesley was not ashamed of the savior. I think he is far happier than we could make him here but that does not help our loss. I _____ to say with David O my son would to God I could die for thee. There is none on earth can tell how I mourn for my dear lost one. If I had known when he was wounded I think I should gone to him but it is all past now and it becomes us to bow to the will of God. I hope my dear that you may be supported in your deep affliction. I trust that the grace of God will enable you to say not my will but thine be done. George wrote me that he was dead but did not tell me when he died nor what he said. I wish that you would send me the particulars and send me your picture. It would be a consolation for me to look upon one that my lovely child loved as I know he did you by his letters to me. Tell Emma to write the particulars about why he is a prisoner. I was in hopes that George would stay at home after he was lame. Don't grieve too much. It will do no good dear Brina. May you long live to bless the world and when our heavenly father shall say come up higher may you meet the dear ones that have gone before where there is no war nor death. Will ever be the prayer of your mother.*

Widows struggle with unfinished business. The government offered a small but useful amount of money called a bounty to each volunteer as an incentive to enlist. Sabrina was forced to try to collect the bounty that was due Wesley upon his enlistment in April 1861. In the letter Wesley wrote after First Manassas, he said that he wanted Sabrina to know that should anything happen to him, he hadn't received a cent from the government since he left Bangor. Apparently he hadn't received the bounty, either, even after more than two months of service.

A year and two months later, Sabrina acted on Wesley's advice and asked her brother-in-law, Charles Brown, to help her get the bounty money so long overdue. Charles wrote back to Sabrina after he consulted a lawyer:

*Bangor Oct 22, 1862*
*Dear Sister*

*I have been to see a lawyer and find that I have got to go through with more forms that I expected (or rather you have). Mr. Crosby has written most of the directions he says that you had better come to Bangor as he says that you cannot get the bounty unless you are here. You will want to get your certificate of marriage and a copy of the same from the town Clerk and bring or send them together with the letter that announced his death. Write as soon as you receive this and let me know when you will be here if you can come and if not write as you receive this.*

*If you wish to sell Wesley's apron and overalls under clothes I will take them and pay you what they are worth. You had better send Wesley's tool chest up as soon as you can as I may get a chance to sell them this fall. Minta and the children are fine.*

It was going to be a major inconvenience for Sabrina to gather the paperwork she would need and then travel to Bangor to claim the money that the government promised to give Wesley a year and a half earlier.

The dead leave things behind. As he was leaving Bangor, Wesley told Brina not to loan his tools to anyone because he planned to build a house for an Islesboro resident in the spring of 1862. That would have meant employment and good money. In October 1861, he mentioned building two other houses as well: "*I hope to get back and build your Brother's house and when 'my ship comes in' I'll build us a home.*" In February 1862, he still held on to this hope and asked Sabrina: "*Have you ever looked into my tool chest since I came away and are the tools rusting?*" Wesley hoped to build houses, establish his reputation as a carpenter on the island, and save enough money to build a house for himself and Sabrina, but that ship didn't come in.

While Sabrina was occupied with the paperwork and things of a former life, she received a letter from a medium. Sabrina did not know the woman personally or as a client, but she had attended two séances in late July 1862. She mentioned the experience in a letter to Luky: "*I went to two spiritual circles this week, quite interesting. It was a trance medium that _____ the spirit of a little Indian girl named Celia Lolah. Chatted with the circle through the medium. I asked her ever so many questions and she answered me; said there were five shirts round me, but I don't believe anything in it.*" We don't know what "Celia" meant when she said that Sabrina had five shirts around her. It may be that the medium saw the clothing of five spirits clustered near her. We recall that by that time in her life, Sabrina had lost five people who were in her immediate family: John and Phebe Seeley, Cordelia, Mighill and Charley. Maybe the shirts represented their spirits. Regardless, Sabrina was not impressed. It may be that a member of that circle thought that Sabrina might consider the services of a medium to ease the ache of her bereavement and so contacted the medium on Sabrina's behalf. Or the medium might have simply been reading the obituaries and regarded Sabrina as a potential client:

*Ellsworth Oct 1862*
*Dear Mrs. Brown*
*You will excuse the liberty I take in thus addressing you but hearing of your bereavement I thought perhaps a word of kindness and sympathy would be agreeable to you stranger 'tho I be dear friend you have my sympathy in this your hour of trial well do I know how hard this is to hear, no matter what our <u>Belief</u> may be it does not remove the fact that our dear ones are gone from us. We cannot see and converse with them as before. We feel that aching void that no Religion can fill. But when we look beyond the wake of tears then it is joy to know they have not left us but only gone before. I can say but little to comfort you for my own heart is full of grief. I expect the Death Angel ere long to take away my dear husband and <u>then</u> and only <u>then</u> when <u>Experience</u> has been my <u>teacher</u> can I fully sympathize with you in your bereavement but my angel friends will never leave me lonely on the way, and dear friend you too will hear the tones of the loved from the angel world bidding you be of good cheer for his spirit is active still and if so will he not seek you. So yes rest assured my dear friend that your dear Husband will make*

known his presence to you and still cheer you while treading life's pathway. I would like to see and converse with you very much yet since that cannot be I thought I would say a few words through the medium of pen and ink. Do not give up too much to your sorrow for "He doeth all things well" and the dear ones are with you and will give you solace in sorrow's hour. A little while and we too shall cross the Mystic River to join the angel band. Oh then let us try to bow in submission and say 'Thy will be done'. Let us draw near to the rod that its way falls lightly upon us. Forgive me if I have intruded too much upon you but I feel we are brothers and sisters of one common Father, and we should seek each other's good. O how much I have been taught of the great Love principle by the dear one in the spirit land and they also tell me when my friends go from me it is but taking up a link of a chain. It not severed but a link has been taken up holding us to the Angel world.

But I must stop now. I have to be entranced in a few moments for a friend now waiting. Excuse this I've written in haste but dear sister I wanted to say a few words to cheer you and may the little that I've said prove of some comfort, and remember this:
He has not left thee sister
But only gone before
To rest his weary nature
Upon the angel shore.

    Yours truly,
    E.S. Thomas

The medium sounds like a spiritual counselor. Her service to Sabrina would have been to offer herself as a conduit between this world and the "angel world," where, presumably, Wesley resides. In a way, she would have been like an envelope in a correspondence, carrying messages back and forth across the "Mystic River." She suggests that mystical conversations between loved ones were a therapeutic form of grief counseling. Religions, she says, do not practice the techniques that can fill the aching void left by the death of a loved one. She might have understood the awkward timing of her letter to a wife so recently widowed, but believed that she could help soothe Sabrina's grieving soul by reassuring her that Wesley was still alive but in a distant, spiritual abode reserved for the blessed. Even George, Sabrina's brother-in-law, said in his letter from Annapolis that he felt that he might yet hear from Wesley, and that he is happy. On the other hand, the medium might have been trying to take advantage of Sabrina's vulnerability.

Nothing more is mentioned about mediums and séances in Sabrina's correspondence. She seemed to prefer the traditional approach to mourning and adapted her wardrobe to suit her mood and society's expectation of her conduct as a widow:

*Castine Oct 24 1862*
*My Dear Sister*
*I will pen you a line this evening in answer to your kind letter which I rec'd, in due time, and also that silk, but I was sorry you sent the brown silk as I fear you may need it, and I have at present no particular use for it, but I used the "black" which is my style for the present and for a few months or years to come...*

After Wesley's death, the tools and the carpenter's apron that Sabrina made held no more meaning, like most of a deceased person's stuff that needs to be distributed, donated, disposed of, or sold after his death. For the living, that process takes time and effort. Sabrina wrote to her sister for help:

*Castine Oct 27/62*
*My Dear Sister*
*It is raining very hard as it has been all day and I'm alone this evening. Thought I would pen you a line as I wished you to do an errand for me if you would and can and it is this: to go over to Capt. G.R. Pendleton and ask him if he will be kind enough to send Wesley's tool chest to Bangor by the first vessel, you might wait until some vessel got in that way going to Bangor and tell him I will settle with him for his trouble, but if you don't like to should not and I will write him a line myself. I would like for you to know what vessel he sends it by so as to write and tell me. Chas Brown wants to sell the tools and I fear they will all spoil if they are not seen to soon. I would come over and see to them myself but I can't come now anyway. I expect I shall have to go to Bangor again soon. I don't know but they have sent for me about some of my business matters. I shant go if I can help it. It costs so much too, cost one four dollars to go and take the stage. But if I go I shall stay some weeks. They want me to come and stay all the fall but I shant I don't think...*

When Sabrina left the island to live with Wesley's relatives, she left his tool chest behind. The tools had value, and money was more useful to Sabrina than a chest of tools that she could not use. Charles, Wesley's brother, bought the tools from Sabrina at a fair price. There was no sense in keeping them for sentimental reasons:

*Bangor Nov 23 1862*
*My very dear sister:*
*...I am ever so much obliged to you for seeing about the toolchest. Capt. Stephen Coombs brought it to Bangor, all safe.*

At this time, a month or so after Wesley's death, Sabrina was living with Emma, her sister-in-law, and she was not inclined to move from there for awhile. From Castine, she wrote her sister, Luky, on Islesboro:

*I will not allude to my great sorrow. It is hidden deep in the recesses of my heart. There let it slumber as sacred from the gaze of the cold world and I trust to time for the healing of the wound...*

She reflected on her own mortality in that same letter as she reacted to the news of the death of an Islesboro girl:

*That was sad about Lovina Coombs. I felt real sorry about it. So young and ___willing to die—Let me prepare. The Death Angel may next bear away my weary spirit to meet the dear ones gone before, 'Be ye also ready'.*

December found Sabrina reluctant to budge from Castine, despite Luky's invitation to visit: "*...but sister I* *should rather not come on to the Island now. It would only awaken and arouse old memories and cause me to feel, if possible, more keenly and deeply my recent great bereavement. The above, dear sister, is the primary reason for not wishing to visit the Island now. I would rather wait until time partially healed the wound..."*

The following spring brought an occasion that would reopen the wound—the return home of the Second Maine:

*Bangor May 22, 1863*
*Dear Sister Luky*
*...The 2nd Regt. Maine Vols. is expected tomorrow. They are going to have a great time here and are going to give then a great dinner at The Norembega Hall. When I think of them coming and know that Wesley is not among them it seems as though I should sink right through the floor. It will be a time of great rejoicing and of great sadness here tomorrow when the 2nd Maine arrives. But Luky it makes me feel so I can't smile about their coming home...*

# SABRINA SEELEY BROWN PENDLETON

After some time, Sabrina recovered. However, tragedy struck again when her sister, Luky, died in June 1866, aged twenty-one, only a couple of years after she married Fields C. Pendleton, thirty-one, an Islesboro ship master and owner. Sabrina married Pendleton, Luky's widower, when she was twenty-six years old. He became prosperous and Sabrina became the mother of eight children. They lived on Islesboro in a house they named Gablewood. Sabrina's daughter Alice founded the Islesboro Free Library and her name is memorialized over the door of that building. Sabrina and Alice shared a trait that made all the difference in the preservation of the story of Wesley and his island wife: They saved things. Sabrina saved letters that preserved a man's life. If she had not done this, all we would know about Wesley would be that his name is inscribed on a bronze plaque that is installed to the left of the front door of the Islesboro library. Alice saved not only her mother's letters, but also the books that gave birth to the collection in the island library. Until the letters were donated to the Islesboro Historical Society, the correspondence that preserves our knowledge of Wesley and Sabrina's life together simply languished.

We can understand why, by the mid-1860s, Sabrina might have felt as if she must be in a perpetual state of spiritual readiness for her own death. "Be ye also ready," wrote Sabrina to her sister a month after Wesley's death. Sabrina borrowed these words from that famous Biblical verse that says that the end of life as we know it will come unexpectedly—like a thief in the night. Surely Sabrina was feeling that the people to whom she was closest were stolen from her without warning. Two years later, when Luky died, Sabrina became the last living member of her family, Robert Nelson having died of yellow fever.

Alice, one of eight of Sabrina's children with Fields Pendleton, never had children to whom she could bequeath family papers. Among the members of her extended family, she was probably the most knowledgeable of the contents of the chest or bags in which the correspondence was stored for so many years. Decades after she died, Pendleton Stevens came into possession of the correspondence and cared enough to donate the letters to the Islesboro Historical Society. Like many historic treasures whose value might seem compromised by a lack of relevance to the present day, they could just as easily have been lost or discarded.

Minta once said that Sabrina would be the means by which a great good would be done in the world, and that good was the nurturing and educating of a daughter who built a social and cultural center that thrives today.

Sabrina and Fields are buried next to each other in the Pendleton family cemetery on the island.

*Sabrina Seeley Brown Pendleton, by this time a mother and wife of Captain Fields Coombs Pendleton. Islesboro Historical Society.*

# EPILOGUE

A war correspondence that contains all of the letters in its collection must be a rare treasure. So many factors assemble to undermine people's best intentions to save their most cherished papers: the loss of a diary on the battlefield, the intentional burning of letters to allow room in a backpack, the theft or failed delivery of mail, the looting of corpses, and the passage of time.

Sabrina saved what she could and this fragmented collection was preserved by conscientious descendents. Sabrina saved a man's life when she vowed to preserve those letters: "Don't take them out of the chest, will you, Luky."

There's a belief that says that at the end of time, the dead will be resurrected, judged, and consigned to one of two places for eternity. In this belief, nobody asks the dead if they want to be resurrected; it simply happens. They are powerless to refuse. Revealing the contents of an old, deeply personal correspondence is like resurrecting the dead without asking their permission. Sentiments and secrets that the correspondents would never have wanted to share with anyone are brought to light for all to read and judge at their leisure. It doesn't seem fair. That is why researching a correspondence is always a privilege and it makes those who are charged with permitting access to old letters mindful of their responsibility to honor the dead.

Some say that a dying person sees his life pass before him. Perhaps Wesley experienced the same. If so, a particular letter, one that Sabrina sent to Wesley while he was living in Auburn, unemployed and feeling unworthy, might have drifted into his fading field of vision, the one at the end of which Sabrina wrote a short poem:

*In pleasures, dreams or sorrow's hour*
*In crowded hall or lonely bower,*
*The object of my life shall be*
*Forever to remember thee.*